YOU WILL NEVER RUN OUT OF JESUS

WILLIAM D. BAILEY, M.D.

CrossHouse

Copyright by William D. Bailey, M.D., 2007
All Rights Reserved
Published by
CrossHouse Publishing,
P.O. Box 461592
Garland, Texas 75046-1592
Printed in the United States of America
by Lightning Source, LaVergne, TN

ISBN 0-929292-24-3

Dedication

I dedicate this book to my wife, Vickie,
who has gone with me on many missions
and supported me on the rest.
She is my sweetest worker and companion.

Foreword

Dr. Bill bounded down the steps of the plane into the thickly blanketed African humidity. He had a surgeon's knife in his back pocket, an adventurous, mischievous glimmer in his eye, and a heart overflowing with Christ's love for all people. Dr. Bill is a regular guy, with white, balding hair, glasses, and a contagious smile. He surrendered to God's direction and through obedience has become more than he ever was or ever thought he could be. He is a man reaching peoples and nations for Christ.

In the African bush, medical clinics held in mud houses with dirt beneath our feet, chickens with chicks crowding our space, and rats running the rafters bring in Voodoo worshipers who might otherwise never hear the truth about forgiveness and life in Jesus Christ. Many medical volunteers have arrived to work with us in Benin over the years, but none have done so as many times as Dr. Bill has. None have had his confidence and amazing skill in MASH-unit type surgery.

We've watched him, with his gentle hands, relieve the extreme pressure of a baby's bladder by correcting a poorly attempted circumcision.

Under brilliant, tropical, green trees and with the bush leaves creating dancing shadows on his head and his feet swimming in the sand, we've witnessed him remove lumps that plagued people for years. Then we've listened to the praises given to Jesus as the patients recuperated while they lay on straw mats.

We've witnessed him, with a zealous compassion to help and heal, puzzle over how to pull a rotted, infected tooth. After a minute's debate with himself he turned to Jeff and asked, "Do you have a pair of pliers in your truck?" Moments later, with pliers covered with antiseptic, the tooth was extracted. The patient grinned with relief.

But Dr. Bill isn't a man going to the nations just to doctor. His surgical abilities simply create a platform from which he shares Jesus. Dr. Bill loves medicine, but he is passionate about the eternal destiny of people—a work Christ performed in his life. He affects people's lives. In every trip to the ends of the globe, each patient's spiritual life is his primary concern. Physical healing is temporary. Knowing Christ is eternal.

We pray that through the pages of this book, a powerful desire to touch the world for Jesus Christ will captivate you.

Barbara and Jeff Singerman
International Board missionaries living in Benin, Africa
Barbara J. Singerman, author of *Beyond Surrender*

Resources

Below are two websites that are valuable resources if you are looking for a mission trip to attend. They list more opportunities than any individual can respond to.

Baptist Medial Dental Fellowship   *www.bmdf.org*

International Mission Board   *www.imb.org*

Acknowledgements

I want to thank all the missionaries I have worked with in 15 different countries. They work tirelessly to spread the Gospel and do the Great Commission.

I would also like to thank my wife, Vickie; my church; and the different pastors that have helped and gone on mission trips with me.

A special thanks goes to the Baptist Medical Dental Fellowship. This group helped me start doing mission work in Asia and Africa.

I offer sincere thanks to my publisher, Catharine L. Moore, and her staff at CrossHouse Publishing for their help and patience with my first efforts to write a book.

Also, I want to thank Dr. Charles Walker, Th.D. who has invited me on several trips to work with his church and LSU medical students from Shreveport.

Table of Contents

Introduction: You'll Never Run Out of Jesus	13
1. My Life Prior to Retirement	15
2. The Experience of Vietnam (August '69 to July '70)	19
3. Further Training	23
4. Private Practice for Almost 25 Years	29
5. Where Heaven and Earth Meet (Israel)	32
6. The Land of Eternal Spring (Guatemala)	41
7. Trip to Mexico with LSU Students	51
8. The Land of the Safari (Kenya)	54
9. Retirement from Private Practice	62
10. The Siam Experience (Thailand)	66
11. Halftime	73
12. Return to the Holy Land May 2000 (Commissioning for My Work)	78
13. The Voodoo Capital of the World (Benin, Africa)	85
14. South Mexico	94
15. Brazil (Teresina and Caxus de Sol) August 2000	99
16. Return to Benin, Africa, June 2001	102
17. Rio de Janeiro (The Beautiful City) November 2001	109
18. The Trip to Maracaibo, Venezuela	115
19. The Land of the Guarani (Paraguay) August 2002 to July 2004	121

20. Return to Rio de Janeiro (August/September 2002)	129
21. North Benin (West Africa) November 2002	134
22. Nicaragua January 2003	141
23. Jamaica June 2003	144
24. Burkina Faso (West Africa) January 2004	148
25. Honduras April 2004	157
26. The Amazon River June 2004, July 2005	162
27. Cambodia November 2004, November 2005	173
28. Return to North Benin January 2005	182
29. The Philippines 2005, 2006	190
30. "Intense and Unrelenting" Ghana April 2006	200
31. The Conclusion of the Whole Matter	209
32. Future Trips Planned, Continuing the Great Commission	210
Photo Album	212
Plan of Salvation	221

Introduction

You'll Never Run Out of Jesus

Most people have never heard the entire story of why I do what I have always wanted to do. This book is written so that the many people I know, have known, and will know can understand why I do what I love to do now.

I had a successful practice in general surgery and family practice, but I became unsatisfied with that practice for several reasons, not because I didn't love people and treating them, but I wanted something even more gratifying in life. I knew I was getting tired of managed care (I call it "Mangled Medicine") and I was nearing burnout because some of my patients were so demanding. I even kidded some of them about joining the diesel-driving academy so I could get away from my demanding practice. I eventually fired the managed care groups (insurance groups) and found that my patients were bound to have to follow their insurance, even though they loved me as a doctor.

Several events happened over a period of approximately two years that eventually made me make the decision to proceed to the second half of my life. I did not know the name for what was happening to me until one of my dear friends called me and told me of the book *Halftime* by Bob Buford. It named the metamorphosis that was already taking place in my life. When Charles Laughridge told me about the book I was already planning to go on a mission trip to Kenya, Africa.

Nevertheless, I immediately ordered a copy from www.amazon.com and read it over the next few days. Now I had a title for the changes that were taking place inside of me and radically altering my life. This involved my wife also, and thank God for a sweet and understanding wife who went through all this with me.

Halftime: Changing Your Game Plan from Success to Significance by Bob Buford was a welcome book and the further advise that I had been searching for. In his book Bob Buford states, "Halftime is time out . . . a time to think seriously about one's purpose in life and draft a game plan for the second half. It is a time when the quest for success loses meaning and you ask 'Is this it?' I've achieved some level of accomplishment, and done much of what I set out to do. What's next? Most call this a 'midlife crisis'. Halftime is a journey . . . a process of transitioning from success to significance that can happen over months to years."

The purpose of this book is to tell the story of how "halftime" has become the last half of life that I have always wanted. I hope to share this ongoing metamorphosis or journey that continues as I write this book. I truly feel that I have gone from success to significance, a life that I want to count toward the most important thing in life to me: Doing the Great Commission (Telling the world about Jesus Christ).

I want this book to be a motivating factor for all who read it. I hope I cause excitement in what I now do, so that you will join me in the most satisfying of job of all: Telling the World about Jesus Christ.

CHAPTER 1

My Life Prior to Halftime

The first half of my life was spent going to school, college, and medical school, completing a medical internship, and doing a tour of duty with the U.S. Navy, including the first year with the Marines in Vietnam. I also received more training during my general-surgery residency. Then for almost 25 years I had my own private practice of surgery and medicine.

One of the memorable questions of my childhood was, "What will I be when I grow up?" As far as I remember I always wanted to be a doctor. My mother encouraged this any time the subject was mentioned. Our family doctor, who birthed all of my siblings and me seemed to be an ideal to follow. He was a family practitioner in solo practice in Converse, Louisiana. I remember how devoted he was to his patients.

In the summer of 1952, my home church, Magnolia Baptist in Hunter, Louisiana, held a revival. Bro. Charles Foxworth was the visiting preacher for the week. On Sunday afternoon of the last day of our revival he visited our home. After talking with the family for a while, he asked to talk with me in private. He asked me if I had Jesus in my heart. I told him I was not sure, so he explained how I could have that saving knowledge. Right then at age 9 and there in my parents' home I prayed to receive Jesus into my heart. That night at church I went forward during the invitation and acknowledged publicly that I had received Jesus into my heart. Two weeks later on a

Sunday afternoon a group of people from our church went to Southside Baptist Church in Mansfield, where a baptistry was available, and all nine of us who during the revival had accepted Jesus were baptized.

I graduated from Stanley High School in May 1961 as valedictorian of my class of fourteen. My mom had been on my case to sign up for college, but I put it off until the last week before the summer session of 1961 started. When I began college, I was placed in the lowest-level classes until my professors determined that I indeed could read and write. I took the college-admission test after I arrived on campus. My advisor attempted to steer me toward a broad education instead of just science courses, but I was stubborn with my own ideas. I ended up with a major in zoology and minors in chemistry and bacteriology. In retrospect, I wish I had listened to the advisor a little closer.

After ten straight semesters without a break I graduated in July 1964 as an honor student from Northwestern State College in Louisiana. Because they were paying for my education, my parents pushed me to finish quickly. I always will be grateful for my dad who worked seven days a week to put his children through school. I was accepted to LSU Medical School in New Orleans and started classes in September 1964. I graduated in May 1968, took (and passed) my Louisiana state-board exams, and headed north to Shreveport where I had been accepted into a rotating internship at Confederate Memorial Medical Center (now LSU Medical School in Shreveport). During that year with the Vietnam War in full swing I felt obligated to do something about the military service. I chose the U.S. Navy through the Berry Plan and went to Dallas, Texas, to be commissioned as a lieutenant in the U.S.Navy.

While there I was being interviewed by Lieutenant JG (a woman) who said I should be happy that the military had allowed me to finish my education prior to entering the service. I informed her that the military had nothing to do with that fact. I told her I was upset that the military was interrupting my training. We got into an argument, and she was proved wrong by a senior officer. As you can imagine, I was not a hit with the military. My superiors asked me if I wanted to be a flight surgeon, a submarine doctor, serve naval-base duty or ship duty, or what. I turned down the flight-surgeon duty as it took extra military training. I preferred not to take the submarine duty, so I was basically left to their mercy.

I finished my internship one day and the next began my travel to Camp Le Jeune, North Carolina, where I had been assigned to the U.S. Marines. Fortunately I had four friends from LSU Med School who took basic training alongside me. Like everyone else, I had no idea what I was truly getting into. To get us ready for Vietnam, we received three to six inoculations daily. One morning I got up and because my arms were so sore had to place my toothbrush in my hand and move my head to brush my teeth. It was nice that we weren't expected to do calisthenics that morning.

One weekend an LSU classmate and I drove to Washington, D.C., and spent the weekend seeing as much as possible of the buildings, memorials, monuments, and museums.

After three weeks we were given travel time to get to Travis Air Force Base in California, the gateway to Vietnam. I drove home to Louisiana, spent several days with my family, and went on a last fishing trip to Toledo Bend Lake. At the end of my stay I flew out of Shreveport where it was 98 degrees *(all temperatures in this book are given in Fahrenheit)*. When I stepped off the plane that night in San Francisco, it was 46 degrees; I thought I was going to freeze.

I went to San Francisco two days early to scope out the area and tour the city, which I had never visited. I had an idea I would return to the Bay area for the second year of my tour of duty when I returned from Vietnam. I saw why the song writer wrote, *I Left My Heart in San Francisco.*

I fell in love with the area and the weather and made up my mind to return there one day.

CHAPTER 2

The Experience of Vietnam

August 1969 to July 1970

Our group left Edwards Air Force Base one evening and landed in Okinawa the next day. We stayed on the island for approximately 24 hours prior to proceeding to Da Nang, Vietnam. I was assigned to the 11th Motor Battalion as the Battalion Aid Surgeon. The hot days of August 1969 were in full swing. I thought I was going to melt the first few days; it was only 98 to 100 degrees, but the humidity was stifling.

I was formally welcomed to Vietnam my fifth night there—the Viet Cong fired rockets and mortar for several minutes. Thank goodness no one on the compound was hurt. We spent the next five nights in bunkers.

I made good friends with my corpsmen and found the duty not so bad. I seldom saw the good Marines but frequently saw those that wanted a medical excuse to get out of something. During my early tenure the H&S (Headquarters and Service) officer tried to run "my show", so I talked to the H&S First Sergeant and he said we would look up our records and evaluate the situation. He determined that the H&S officer was really a Warrant Officer given the rank of Captain (Marines) while in country (Vietnam). I was a First Lieutenant (same as Captain in the Marines) but given time for college, medical school, and internship training. So I outranked him. Also the

First Sergeant told me I was the third-ranking officer in the company; only the CO and XO were superior to me. He said, "Besides these are people you don't fool with: the CO, XO, the ones that pay you, the ones that feed you, and then the doctor.

He told me, "Those two bars on your shoulder are railroad tracks; use them." I had no further administrative problems during my stay there.

One day the Captain of Transportation and Social Services asked if a few of my corpsmen and I would like to be transported to a nearby village for a med-cap (medical civilian aid program). I readily agreed; three days later we were in the village with two interpreters and two Marines with rifles for security. The med-caps went so well we soon were going twice weekly to this village. I found the villages and countryside to be just beautiful; the lush rice fields in various stages of maturity were like a large green quilt of varying shades. The landscape was completed with multiple banana trees and grass huts where the villagers lived. The people were friendly, and we were well received. I wondered why we were at war with people like this. They were so appreciative and grateful. I became friends with several of the villagers.

Eventually we went to the villages three to five days weekly. Our captain was praised for our efforts, and we loved doing the work—it was a labor of gratitude. (My, how I wish I had been evangelical as I am now. So many people there needed the Lord, and I didn't think of it at the time).

One day I was asked by the captain to go to the home of a dying South Vietnamese soldier. The fellow had been sent home to die because his diarrhea and other maladies would not respond to their local hospital treatments. I had the soldier brought to our Battalion Aid Station. I started him on IV fluids and Chloromycetin (something I didn't usually use on the

Marines because of inherent dangers). The soldier improved so much in two days he was able to return to his village and later back to military service. Before leaving the soldier dropped by my office and wanted to pay me, so I accepted a tall bamboo tree (I didn't realize it was very valuable to them). I took the pole, cut it in sections divided by the septae, took off the superficial covering, and with an electric cautery etched each with a scene of Vietnam and the surrounding compound. (I still have these as a memento of Vietnam).

Another day I was busy with the Marines and failed to go to see a sick young Vietnamese girl. I would have needed special permission and security to go out into the village, so I just let the moment pass. Two days later one of the village people told me, with tears in his eyes, that the young girl had died the previous night. I should have taken the initiative to go there or have her brought to me. I determined that I would try harder to see people like her the next time. I knew it was an honor to be asked in the first place.

On another occasion I was requested to cross the street to the 1st Motor Battalion Aid Station, where I was also the Battalion Aid Surgeon. There I found a middle-aged Vietnamese male who had been bitten by a Cane snake. His legs were swollen massively and the edema was also pronounced in his lower abdomen. Amazingly his vital signs were normal. I proceeded to give him twelve amps of Antivenin (Crotalidae) Polyvalent. I was told that this snake was known as a twelve-step snake—take twelve steps and you're dead. I believe in miracles and prayer. I have no medical reason to explain why this man should have lived; he should have died in anaphylactic shock or renal shutdown. But, he didn't. Instead within hours the swelling started to go down and he became progressively better. By the third day he went home a happy man with only a mild residual from the snake bites. It was a miracle and an answer to prayer. I initially did not believe he would live.

Before long because such a need existed, I started literally pulling teeth. I began with a gloved hand and gauze, then graduated to a hemostat. I still was breaking off some teeth, so I went to the battalion dentist who agreed to accompany me and do the dental work. I saw the medical patients and he saw the dental patients. We became best friends.

On Christmas Day 1969 I received orders that I was being assigned to the 2nd Marines, 5th Battalion in An Hua, 20 miles northeast of Da Nang. I transferred there and made good friends with the corpsmen again. Soon after arriving I asked my CO (commanding officer) if I could go into the surrounding villages to do med-caps. He agreed and sent me with the blessings of transportation, supplies, and security. We earned the respect of the community by our service.

While there I visited Hill 55 where Sgt. Carlos Hathcock did much of his duty as the "Silent Warrior", a very famous Marine Sniper. But by then it was a safe place to trek.

I fairly frequently flew in the different helicopters, the CH-47 (mostly a transport helicopter), the Huey (my favorite), and the CH-53E Super Stallion.

On one occasion I was asked by my CO to accompany him to the field where we were expected to see only light action. I was told to bring my medical supplies to treat the people out in the field. The day was hot and humid; I blistered in the light shade of a tree. We spent two days and two nights near one of the local rivers. The people were appreciative once again. The med-cap was now a measure of good will. I still loved it.

The year went fast in some aspects, especially the enjoyable part of doing the med-caps in the nearby villages. I determined that year that some day I wanted to do this often or full time.

Chapter 3
Further Training

While in Vietnam I often thought of what further training I would pursue when I finished my tour of duty with the U.S. Navy. Because I felt I needed more training before going in private practice, I had turned down doing general practice in Mansfield, Louisiana, with Dr. Jack Grindle. I kept thinking over and over that the best program where I took my internship at Confederate Memorial Medical Center was the general-surgery residency.

As my first choice to finish the second year of my tour of duty I had applied for the Oakland Naval Hospital in Oakland, California. I was given priority for that since I had served in Vietnam. I started home after 360 days in Vietnam. I felt stranded in Okinawa for three-and-one-half days. I had planned to go to Hong Kong and/or Taipei so I could buy some silk suits on the way home, but I couldn't get a flight out to either, so I came back to Los Angeles, then on to Shreveport.

I visited a few days, then Tommy, my brother, and I started out for Oakland, California. We went through Dodge City, Kansas, then on to Denver and the Rockies, then to the Grand Canyon, and on to Las Vegas, and finally to San Francisco, where Tommy took a flight home. I proceeded to Oakland to find an apartment for the year.

I liked the Naval Hospital in Oakland, especially the 16

hours I had off every day and three weekends off each month. I spent several long weekends with one of my LSU Medical School classmates, Randy Kirchner, M.D., and one of his friends, Marvin Sachs, M.D. They were in Vietnam at the same time I was. We went to Disneyland, snow skiing at Squaw Valley and the Ski Ranch near Lake Tahoe, Nevada, and Yosemite National Park. It was a great place to visit and have fun, but I had determined I wanted to return home. I had applied and been accepted to the general-surgery residency at Confederate Memorial Medical Center in Shreveport.

While in California I applied for and received privileges through reciprocity to work (moonlight) while I was in Oakland. I started off by flying from Oakland to Los Angeles for a couple of weekends and working in two of the hospitals near the Los Angeles airport. The last weekend I worked for forty-eight hours with a hospital that had a contract with the Los Angeles Police Department. I had time to eat twice and take one shower. I was leaving, but no one came to relieve me, and people involved in a major motor vehicle accident were arriving soon, so, I agreed to work another twenty-four hours. It was tough, but I got a lot of good experience in the emergency room. That weekend I treated sixteen Red Devil (Seconal, a barbiturate) overdoses and one Angel Dust (a strong hallucinogenic) overdose—and that was an experience! I unfortunately also had to treat a few rape cases.

Shortly afterwards I sought and found a job at a local hospital in Hayward, the St. Rose Hospital. I was offered a full-time job there, but about that time I received the good news of my acceptance to the general-surgery program at Confederate.

I enjoyed my year in California, but I ignored a major thing, church. I was always off having fun, but I missed going to Sunday School and church on a regular basis. I determined to start again soon.

I drove the long path back from Oakland to Shreveport in two days and soon began the demanding days of general-surgery residency. Rounds started at 5 a.m. Two of the four first-year residents were still in the military for two more months. Because of this, the other resident and I had to work thirty-six hours on and twelve hours off for those two months.

I had just arrived from the pleasant weather in Oakland and the Bay Area where it was 44 to 55 degrees at night and 55 to 70 during the day. Shreveport in July is hot and humid, just like Vietnam. Again I almost melted; in those days there was little or no air conditioning at Confederate Memorial Medical Center. I must have drunk a gallon of orange juice every night for the first month to keep hydrated and for energy.

It was a real learning experience. Four days into my surgery residency—on July 4th—we had so many gunshots, stabbings, and major blunt traumas from motor-vehicle accidents that all the other surgery residents were in the operating rooms, while I was doing all the triage, treatment, and preparations to get them ready for surgery. That was an all-day and all-night duty for sure. The long days and nights went by fairly quickly.

One day as I was leaving from work I saw the most gorgeous, slim blonde I had ever seen. It was love at first sight. It took me three days to find out who she was. Finally, one of the clerks on the surgery ward found out her name and where she worked. Within the next day or so I was walking from the emergency room to the library with a freshly killed snake. I needed to find out by looking it up in an encyclopedia or medical reference if it was poisonous. Just before entering the library that pretty blonde walked by with two of her friends. I asked them if they would like to see my snake, and they were curious enough to look. I had found out that the gorgeous blonde worked in Social Service next to the library. I got up the nerve to call Social Service and ask for her by name: Vickie Chandler. I asked her to go down the hall to the telephone by the emergency room. We got into a conversation and before she knew it, I had asked her out for a date—on a Wednesday night no less. Well, the Chandlers were church folks and the parents told her she would have to go to church before going out on a date on Wednesday nights.

I traveled to Haughton and met her parents. I wanted to impress her, so we went to Sansone's Italian Restaurant (just about the fanciest restaurant in town).Vickie was actually too nervous to eat much, even the special dessert, flamed baked Alaskan—but she was impressed; for sure I was.

Every free night I tried to take her out. Even her mother said I was crowding her, but I knew I had a good thing and I wouldn't let go. Within four months we were engaged and married within another four.

The surgery residency seemed to go easier because I had a sweet wife at home. The rotation through the V. A. Hospital seemed tailor-made for a young, freshly married couple. Although I have very fond memories of our apartment at Villa del Lago on Cross Lake, we soon had a new home. We purchased a house in Bossier City in July 1972 and have been in the city since. I have always claimed that Vickie's umbilical cord was short and we couldn't move away, but it was really home for me too. We joined Airline Baptist Church in 1972 soon after we moved to Bossier City and since then have been members there all but a few years.

Unfortunately Vickie had two miscarriages before we were truly blessed by having our first child, a son named Brian. I will always remember the night our son was born; I found out first and rushed back to tell her parents, "I got my boy!"

The second and third year of surgery residency continued

to roll by. My first week as fourth-year surgery resident was very memorable. I had to repair three subclavian artery injuries—often a very difficult and demanding surgical procedure.

One of my favorite stories happened one Friday night, the shoot-em up night. I was rotating through pediatric-surgery service. I had been treating three children who were burned very badly in a natural-gas explosion in their home. I had been trying to get them transferred to the San Antonio Burn Center, but it had no openings at the time. That night I was called to ER about a gunshot victim. The paramedic told me that this dude just got out of prison the day before and was at a local bar and one of his "friends" shot him with a 45-caliber pistol. The bartender looked at this guy and stated that he was still alive. The shooter came back across the room and shot him five more times. On arrival the patient was agonal; he was taking his last breath or two. He proceeded to die quickly. His mom arrived to the ER soon and became very despondent over the death of her son. I proceeded to tell her that even in this depressing moment that her son could really help someone. I told her of the three children on the pediatric ward that needed a homograft for burns; in fact, I took her up to the ward and showed her the children and their needs. She agreed to allow me to take homografts from her son and help the children. For the next three hours Dr. Tommy Mook and I took all the skin we could from the victim in the operating room under sterile conditions. Later that morning I painstakingly placed all the homograft on the three children's burns. Miraculously two of the children did so well they did not need any further treatment; they healed completely as the homograft sloughed off. For expeditious reasons we proceeded to do minor skin grafts on the third so he could go home soon with his brother and sister.

One busy Sunday afternoon I got a call from E.A. Conway Hospital in Monroe that they had a guy who had been stabbed in the heart with a knife. They had a small percutaneous catheter in his pericardium to relieve the cardiac tamponade. They wanted to transfer him to us, but one of the other residents told them to get out their textbook and perform the surgery. Anyway, he was transferred to us and we rapidly prepared him for the operating room. On exploration he had a small laceration of his anterior descending artery. I repaired that and the surgery was completed. For some reason I seemed to have bumped my head on the top of the door frame as I left the operating room.

I guess my favorite story would be the time Dr. Wayne Sessions called me at home just before our residency was up (we were allowed to stay at home if less than fifteen minutes away). He said he had a guy that had been shot in the neck and was aspirating and coughing up blood with every breath. I arrived and the anesthetist was trying to intubate him but couldn't see the vocal cords for all the blood. I told her to let me have the endotracheal tube. I was very fortunate in getting it down on first attempt. I said, "Now he's mine." We explored his neck and he had almost severed his common carotid artery and was bleeding into the hypopharynx. We repaired that and explored the other side. He had only injured his internal jugular vein; this was easily repaired. The patient did well and went home in four days.

Before the end of my fourth year in surgery residency I had decided to stay in Bossier City. I was having difficulty finding office space, but found an old house on Benton Road about one mile from my home. My father-in-law just happened to be a carpenter, so he repaired and fixed the place for a doctor's office.

Chapter 4

Private Practice for Almost 25 Years

Although not openly welcomed I found a niche at Bossier Medical Center and started my practice the day after I completed my general-surgery residency.

I was thrilled to have six patients the first day. My first patient was Louis Humphrey; he persuaded my secretary to put his name ahead of the first lady who had called a couple of days earlier and scheduled an appointment. It is ironic that my last patient after almost twenty-five years was his son, Cooksey Humphrey. After seeing these patients my father-in-law and I finished pouring the concrete to complete my parking lot in the back of my office.

I took general-surgery call at Bossier Medical Center and asked special permission to take general-medical call, which was gladly given away by the older staff members: Drs. McCuller, Martin, Reichman, and Forbing. You would be surprised at how many surgical cases came out of medical call.

Soon I got permission as a courtesy staff physician at Schumpert Medical Center to take general surgery call there. Some days or weekends I was on call at both hospitals and went from one hospital to the next doing surgery. I even went to the Schumpert Medical Center ER after midnight many nights to suture lacerations, etc. until the ER finally got full time ER doctors.

I built my practice the old fashion way: I worked at it daily.

I will never forget the first surgery I did as a private practitioner. A resident from Vivian called and asked if I could amputate a child's toe that had been cut under a lawn mower. In the operating room I tried and was fortunate to be able to place all the pieces back together and wire the bone. Amazingly he healed nicely, but had a stiff toe for a long time.

In 1976 Vickie and I were blessed with another arrival, our daughter, Julie, who was born in September. She was tiny, weighing in at 5 pounds and 3 ounces. It seemed as if I could hold her in the palm of my hand. Sadly, Vickie miscarried two more times after Julie's birth.

After nearly five years at my location at 822 Benton Road in Bossier City I was fortunate to obtain a lot on Doctors Drive adjacent to Bossier Medical Center. I was so proud when I finally moved into my new office. The night before I started in my new office I personally took every one of my medical records to my new office so they would not be misplaced. My practice thrived in the new location and with hard work. I was still in solo practice; I had looked for a partner but could not find one. I even built the new office for two doctors.

About the time my office was completed a financial crunch occurred involving interests rates; I couldn't seem to get a permanent mortgage. Luckily one of my patients was a banker. He allowed me to pay floating notes depending on the interest rate. That was the period when the rates went to 22%; that meant I was briefly paying 24% interest rate on my loan. Needless to say I paid off the loan as soon as possible.

Finally in 1982 Dr. Bipin Turakhia moved into my office for approximately a year; then he built himself a new office up the street. He is still a good friend and remains Vickie's and my private doctor.

Many memorable cases and patients occurred over the years. I met so many people who became my friends. I couldn't go anywhere in town that people didn't cordially greet me when they saw me out in public.

Changes occur with time. In 1995 James Elrod came to town. After Bossier Medical Center turned down his offer to buy the hospital, he built a new hospital and office building. He gathered the area doctors and offered us a great deal. He wanted us to sell our offices to him, and he would lease us an office in his new building for a minimum of ten years. I took the tour to Baton Rouge General Hospital with him on his private plane and was impressed by him and his offer. It really would have been a wise business investment. I declined what was probably the greatest business offer I've ever received. I wanted to retire in less than ten years.

As it turned out I eventually did retire from private practice after the Willis Knighton Bossier Hospital opened. Although I was on the staff there for almost three years. I had a bigger plan in life than working in private practice until retirement.

By 1998 I was growing weary of managed care (I call it "mangled medicine"). After a few lawsuits, which occasionally come along, I decided to drop general surgery and just do general practice. Doing just general practice was not satisfying like general surgery had been. I truly missed doing surgery. Nevertheless, I dropped my surgery privileges in all the hospitals where I was a staff member.

Chapter 5

Where Heaven and Earth Meet Israel

December 1998

During several conversations with my good friend, Dr. John Miciotto, we decided to visit Israel. I had called a travel agency and received information about the trip when one of Vickie's aunts, Jean Kruithof, told us to call Rev. Mike Gilchrist in Shreveport. Mike was going to the Holy Land soon for the 37th time. So I called and quickly became friends with Mike. He was so cordial and pleasant. Vickie had not planned to go with us until one evening while I was away working. Mike called and during the conversation he told her that the only problem of going to Israel would be getting to the Shreveport airport from Bossier City. He told her that Israel was safer than Bossier City or Shreveport. He said she could walk down an Israeli street at 3 a.m. and be safe. He, not I, convinced her to go with us. Unfortunately after all of this Dr. Miciotto decided not to go.

We left December 28, 1998, and arrived in Germany the next morning. While in the airport there we met some new friends who now have become life-long friends, especially Charles and Gayle Laughridge from Clarkdale, Georgia, outside of Atlanta. We met in the airport in Germany; Vickie and

Gayle are so much alike, it is like they were born sisters. We also met two of their friends, Ty and Beth Tyner, also from near Atlanta. The four had become friends a year earlier during another trip with Mike.

We went to the Koln (pronounced like colon) Cathedral in Cologne, Germany. History says it took 632 years to build. They began building the cathedral in 1248 in order to house the relics of the three Magi. After completing three sections, the work was halted and not resumed until 1823. It was finished in 1880, true to the Gothic style and the original plans. It survived the World War II bombings. It was a magnificent building you could see from miles away. We went to the Rhine River by the city of Bompart and boarded a boat and cruised down the river seeing several medieval castles, grape vineyards, and towns.

After a thorough search we boarded an El Al plane and headed for Tel Aviv. We arrived there Dec. 29th. We stayed in a hotel in Herzlia, a town on the Mediterranean Sea. We took a stroll down the beach the next morning. We met our Jewish tour guide for the rest of the trip, Allen Marks. He was originally from Great Britain. We traveled north along the Sharon Valley to Caesarea. Usually that area of the country receives 16 inches of rain a year. That day it rained a total of 8 inches. We saw the Roman Theater in Caesarea, then the Aqueduct of Caesarea built by the Romans before the time of Jesus. We think that things are old in the U.S. if they are 100 years old, but in Israel things are old if they are more than 1,000 to 3,000 years old.

We made our way to Haifa passing fields of bananas and various citrus fruits. We ascended to the top of Mount Carmel. It rained so hard we could barely make out the Jezreel Valley below. We saw the statue of Elijah and the spot where he challenged the 450 prophets of Baal. Our Israeli guide gave us a talk (sermon) on Elijah and Baal. "If the Lord is God, follow Him! But if Baal is god follow him." For eight hours the prophets of Baal tried to burn the sacrifice, but no fire came. They even cut themselves, but there was no reply from their gods. Elijah made an altar and even wet the wood with four barrels of water three times. Elijah walked up to the altar and prayed. Fire flashed down from heaven and burned up everything, even the water in the ditch around the sacrifice. Then Elijah took all the prophets to Kishan Brook and killed them there. (Summarized from 1 Kings 18:22-40)

Then we traveled to the Meggido excavations; this is where they sacrificed babies to Baal. The place is approximately 5,000-years old. The numerous battles fought there made it a symbol of war. Christian tradition envisions that the last and great battle of the world will be fought at Meggido (Armaggedon). *And he gathered them together into a place called in the Hebrew tongue: Armaggedon.* (King James Bible: Revelation 16:16) This is where the rulers of the world will fight the last great battle between good and evil. The large open plain looks beautiful at this point in time, but that will change as described in the Book of Revelation.

We went 120 feet down the water tunnel, which was extended to a stream outside the city. We saw the remnants of Ahab's chariot city where stables for 450 horses and 150 chariots were located. The rain continued, but it did not dampen our spirit of wanting to take in all this. It was like looking through a history book.

Next we went to Nazareth, the city where Jesus grew up. The streets were narrow for the bus. It was still misting rain, but we could still see the Church of the Annunciation in the distance. This is where the angel Gabriel told Mary she would be the mother of Jesus. According to our tour guide, Nazareth has been and remains the most peaceful city in Israel where Jews, Christians, and Arabs live in near harmony.

Outside of Nazareth was Mount Tabor, called the Mount of Transfiguration which we read about in Luke 9:28-36 where Jesus took Peter, James, and John up the mountain to pray.

As he was praying, Jesus appeared in glory; his raiment was white and glistening, and his face shining as the sun. Then two men appeared and began talking with them; Moses and Elijah. They were splendid in appearance, glorious to see, and they were speaking of his death at Jerusalem.

We spent the next two nights near the city of Tiberias, which is on the northern edge of the Sea of Galilee. The first night in Tiberias our small group of six—Ty and Beth Tyner, Charles and Gayle Laughridge, Vickie and I—were finishing a sumptuous buffet meal. The vegetables and fruit were the best I have ever eaten; they are vine ripened when harvested. Ty told us that he wanted to share his testimony with us. (The Tyners and the Laughridges had made the tour the previous year with Mike GilChrist.)

Ty told us that while they were at the Garden of Gethsemane the previous year and while listening to a sermon, that as clear as day Jesus appeared to him and pointed to him and said,

"Go witness for me." He said he had not been the same since, and every day that he doesn't tell at least 10 people about Jesus he is miserable. There was not a dry eye at our table, as tear drops fell like a spring shower.

I was so touched by Ty's testimony I couldn't get his story off my mind. I thought that if Jesus could change him so much he could change me too. I prayed for a long time that night. I told Jesus that I knew I was His child from my previous salvation experience, but not a true servant. I asked Jesus to let His will be mine. I wanted to surrender my life and services to Him—whatever that would be. Just show me the way, I prayed. Things did not happen immediately, but over the next year or so my life was changed forever. It seems that when you give your service to Him, things do indeed change. The remainder of this book will give evidence to that.

The tour continued the next morning. From our bus we had a view where the Jordan River enters the Sea of Galilee. We then went on to Capernaum, the city of Jesus; it was also the home of St. Peter. The flowers there were just beautiful; the Bougainvillaea were the prettiest I have ever seen. There we saw the remains of Peter's home—a church is now built over most of that site. This was where Jesus healed Peter's mother of a malady and she proceeded to serve them a meal.

Down the street were the remnants of the church over the site where Jesus preached. The outline of the church is still fully intact as well as where that church was built over an earlier one.

Not far away is the Church of the Mount of the Beatitudes. In 1937 the Franciscans built the church, which was funded by Mussolini. From there we could see the site where Jesus gave the Sermon on the Mount.

We then boarded a ship and went out on the Sea of Galilee. The ship stopped in the middle of the Sea. Mike Gilchrist asked us to close our eyes, listen and picture Jesus walking on the water. What a beautiful, serene, and peaceful moment that was! He then gave a talk about Jesus and the Galilee Sea.

Then we journeyed to the Jordan River where several of our group were re-baptized in the cool waters at the baptistry. I mentioned to Vickie that I felt the need to be baptized again because of my talk with Jesus the previous night, but I let it pass. I determined if I were ever there again I would be baptized symbolically for my new service that I had promised.

The next morning we went to the city of Hatzar, one of Solomon's fortified cities. It had been buried by an earthquake and only had recently been excavated.

We then went to the Springs of Gideon, where in the book of Judges, Gideon had carefully chosen his 300 soldiers to fight the Midianites. Allen, our tour guide, told us Gideon chose only those who lapped water from their left hands as they looked about them.

On the road to Jericho we saw orange, lemon, grapefruit, and date trees plus several other kinds of fruit and vegetables. The Israelis use an irrigation system called drip irrigation for their plants. The Jordan River frequently stays low because so much water is removed from the river for that irrigation. The Jordanians across the river also use this technique.

Jericho is one of the oldest cities in the world. There we were shown what is believed to be the original remnant of the walls of the city of Jericho. Nearby is the Mount of Temptation where Satan tempted Jesus.

Next we went by Qumran where the Dead Sea Scrolls were found in a cave in 1947. Not too far along the road was Masada, a mountain 2,000 feet above the level of the Dead Sea, which is the lowest point on Earth. According to our guide, the Dead Sea—which easily could be seen from Masada—had shrunk about 20% to 25% over the last two decades because so much water was being taken from the Jordan River which empties into the Dead Sea. There is no outflow from the Dead Sea.

The next two days we spent exploring the cities of Jerusalem and Bethlehem. Leaving Jerusalem and going into Bethlehem was like going into a different country. There was an astounding difference in the Palestinian territory; there had been talk about turning this area, including Bethlehem and Jericho, over to the Palestinians. We visited the Church of the Nativity, the location where Jesus was said to have been born.

From there we went to see the statue of St. Jerome and the room where he translated the Bible into Latin from Greek and Hebrew. He did this for job security for the priests as they were the only ones who could read or speak Latin at that time.

Next we visited the Holocaust Museum. It was very touching and leaves no doubt as to the reason the museum was built.

The following morning we went to Mount Zion (the beautiful city of God) and into the old walled City, seeing the Tower of David on the way. We proceeded to the Western Wall (Wailing Wall). This is the only remnant of the second temple. This is the Jews' holiest site. Many visit there daily to pray, meditate, and read the Scriptures. Barmitzvahs are held there frequently. This is a ceremony or celebration held when a Jewish boy becomes thirteen years old to affirm that he has reached the age of religious responsibility.

Immediately above the Wall is the Dome of the Rock, the Muslim's third most holy shrine. We didn't get to go in as there was such a long waiting line. Time is everything on a tour where you are out to see and learn all you can.

Then we walked over to the Pool of Bethseda, where Jesus healed the lame man on the Sabbath. Adjacent to this was the Church of St. Ann; while there our group got to sing *Hallelujah*. The sound was unbelievable because of the acoustics and enormity of the church.

From there we went to the Upper Room. This is a huge open room capable of holding 300 to 400 people fully packed. Our group sang: *There's a Sweet Sweet Spirit in This Place*.

We then walked to the Antonio Fortress. Jesus had been condemned by the Sanhedrin, led from the House of Caiphus, and brought to the Antonia Fortress. It was here that he was mocked, scourged, crowned with thorns, and condemned to death. The carvings on the stones there are the actual carvings of the games the Roman soldiers played while Jesus was being condemned to die.

Even though the Via Dolorosa was crowded we retraced the steps of Jesus carrying His cross, stopping at some of the stations to read of the events that took place there on the way to the Holy Sepulchre Church.

Next we walked outside the walled city to the Church of Gethsemane. We went inside and saw the Rock of Agony where Jesus often prayed. As I prayed there it was such an emotional moment. It was like praying next to where Jesus actually was at that moment.

Passing the almost 2,000-year-old olive trees we made our way into the Garden of Gethsemane. Our guide had reserved an area for us where we had a service and sang *Sweet Hour of Prayer*.

We then proceeded in our bus to the top of the Mount of Olives and viewed all of the old city. What a magnificent view! Our group then walked down the hill through the Jewish cemetery to the Dominis Flevit (the Lord Wept) Church. The church was built in 1891 and designed to resemble a tear shaped shrine.

Next we went to the St. Peter in Gallicantu Church; it was here where Peter denied Jesus three times. In the church we went down to an old dry cistern called The Pit. Here Jesus was held captive for a few hours. It was designed as a place where a condemned criminal could not escape. The prophecy was read by Mike Gilchrist from Psalm 88. Mike gave such a touching sermon of what Jesus did for us that by the end we all had tears.

The Garden Tomb was at the edge of a beautifully manicured garden. As we walked into the tomb in small numbers it was a bit larger than I imagined. The best thing about the tomb was that it was empty because Jesus lives. As we went out the door we saw a plaque that read: *He is no longer here for He has arisen.*

Israel truly is where Heaven and Earth meet. What a wonderful trip. I had gone there in a spiritual mindset, but never dreamed that I had found what I had really wanted all along: To follow and serve the Lord in the manner of the Great Commission. My life began to change from that time forward and is still evolving.

Chapter 6

The Land of Eternal Spring Guatemala

1999-2003

The first year nurse Carolyn Freeman asked me about donating supplies and medicines for a medical mission trip to Guatemala I didn't think too much of it. The following year I specifically asked her where, what, when, and why. She told me that Health Talents International (HTI) made a semi-annual trip to Chocola, Guatemala, to do general and gynecological surgery. She told me that this was the oldest continuing group that sponsors missions to Guatemala and Nicaragua. People from all over the US belong to this group.

The Health Talents International, Inc. website states:
"Founded in 1973 in Birmingham, Alabama, Health Talents International is a non-profit Christian organization that works within the Churches of Christ to promote medical evangelism in developing countries.

"As Christians, we feel that God expects us to use our talents, medical and otherwise, in His service. (Matthew 25)"

HTI ministry operates a Christian hospital, conducts daily mobile medical/dental clinics in many different villages. They are staffed by Guatemalan and U.S. health professionals. In addition, every year teams of physicians, nurses, and a variety of non-medical personnel travel at their own expense to Guatemala to work side by side with the Guatemalan staff to meet the medical and surgical needs of the Guatemalan people. Through this medical-evangelism ministry, the HTI have helped establish ten churches in the past three years (2002-2004), and reflected the compassion of Christ to more than 15,000 souls in 2004.

HTI developed and operates the first Church of Christ surgical facility in the western hemisphere. In February 2002 HTI dedicated a brand new modern facility called Clinica Ezell. It consists of three surgical suites, a 50-bed ward, clinic exam rooms, pharmacy, lab, and X-ray room. Adjacent to the surgical center is a dormitory that houses 50 visiting-team members, a large commercial kitchen and dining area.

The website gives the Health Talents objectives:

To proclaim the Gospel in both word and deed through teaching and providing health care.

To train indigenous people as Christian health promoters in their home communities.

To provide opportunities for Christians to use their talents in service to God.

The above information was supplied by Marie Agee, long time coordinator for HTI; she has been most helpful in all our trips. If it weren't for her, things would surely not go as smooth as they do now. She has the heart of a true missionary.

In 1997 I finally consented to go and convinced my wife, Vickie, to go also on the February 1998 surgical clinics. We were all signed up, paid up, and ready to go, but a group on a bus from the University of Maryland was stopped on Coastal Highway in Guatemala where we were going. They were robbed, and several of the women were raped by the armed bandits. The group prayed about it and HTI decided to let us proceed with our trip, but a couple of weeks before we were to leave for Chocola, Guatemala, gunfire in the village due to political instability, caused the U.S. Embassy in Guatemala to call off all medical missions at that time. Our group from the Bossier City/Shreveport area was sorely disappointed, but we determined to go the next year.

By the following year all seemed calm in Guatemala. HTI invited a group to go on the general and gynecological surgery clinic in February, 1999. Vickie had other commitments at that time, but I decided to go with a group from the Bossier City/Shreveport area. Our group consisted of Rod Hyatt, C.R.N.A., Carolyn Freeman, R.N., Vicki Ratts, R.N. (also a board member of HTI), Lynea Hollis, R.N., and me.

Medical and surgical supplies and medicines were readied. We obtained our airplane tickets through the efforts of HTI coordinator Marie Agee. I found Marie to be very helpful and cordial with all the arrangements and preparation for the trip.

Boarding the airplane at Shreveport, we flew to Houston, met the rest of our group, then flew to Guatemala City, arriving after 10 p.m. After gathering all our luggage and supplies we rode via bus to a nearby seminary where dormitory rooms were available for us. Approximately five hours of rest is a short night. We had to rise and shine and be on the bus by 6 a.m. We were told that we would not stop enroute to Chocola because of the recent past circumstances.

On arrival at the HTI clinic we were welcomed by a large, delicious breakfast, including papaya, pineapple, and other local fruits. These fruits were some of the best I have ever eaten. Homemade tortillas with our eggs complemented our meal. We were told to fill our solar shower bags with water and put them out in the sun if we wanted warm showers that night. Also we were instructed not to flush any toilet paper in the commodes as this would clog the drainage system there.

The HTI clinic was an old coffee factory and processing station for locally grown coffee. The coffee-processing plant had used only water power in its operation. It was one of a kind. People traveled from all over the world to see it in operation. Our dormitory was in one section. The outpatient clinic was in another where the coffee research had been done in the past. The other building was for two operating rooms and a surgical ward capable of holding about 28 patients. Fortunately we had air conditioning for the operating rooms. At the rear of this was a large assortment of supplies donated by doctors, nurses, and various groups participating in medical missions.

Dr. Sergio Castillo was waiting at breakfast for us. He is a native Guatemalan doctor hired by HTI to treat the local people and to help with all the clinic work. He invited us to the outpatient clinic so we could ready patients for surgery. Most of the general-surgery patients had hernias of one type or the other. Most gynecological surgical cases were prolapsed uteri.

The surgeons were Danny Lee Minor, M.D., also a board member of HTI, Chris Porter, M.D., a surgical resident, Bob Threkeld, M.D., a retired general surgeon, and me. The gynecologists were Roy Kellum, M.D. and Robin McGuire, M.D. The anesthesiologists were Jeff Bennie, M.D., also an HTI board member, and David Netterville, M.D. Rod Hyatt, C.R.N.A., was our nurse anesthetist.

Our group evaluated the waiting patients. As soon as we could, we started performing procedures in the operating room. The surgeons rotated in turns so each would get the same number of cases. Almost all of the cases were done with spinal anesthesia. The second day we operated until after 8 p.m. One night the electricity went out and we had to operate by flashlight until we got our small generator going, then finished by 11 p.m.

On Sunday evening when the surgery cases were complete, we went to the Santa Thomas Church of Christ services. People in the U.S. would be upset if services were longer than two hours; here the service had just gotten warmed up after two hours. It lasted until 9 p.m., almost five hours. We had two sermons, the Lord's Supper and several songs. The music and singing in Spanish were just beautiful. One female teenager had the most beautiful voice; she towered above all the rest with her singing. In retrospect, I wish I had been a music scout or talent agent, so she could have been hired on the spot.

Every day our group would arise early and as soon as possible start seeing patients at the out-patient clinic for evaluation for surgery. Dr. Castillo had already found these patients in his different clinic sites and referred them here for surgery. Some of these patients had walked up to ten miles or rode the bus to the clinic and had arrived as early as 5 a.m. The people were very friendly and always had a smile, especially when you would greet them with *buenos dias* (good morning) first.

The days went by very fast. If we finished before dark a group of us would walk to the center of the village of Chocola. The folks there were very friendly also. Many German people lived and worked in the coffee industry in the village of Chocola prior to World War II. After the war, things changed and most of them left. Old warehouses near the center of the village reminded us of their presence. The aqueduct that was built prior to 1941 was still intact and brought cool, fresh water down from the nearby mountains.

The surrounding mountains, which covered half of the horizon, had been formed by volcanoes that had long been inactive. Banana trees, coffee plants, and papaya trees were everywhere. The whole landscape was like a lush green garden.

Every night we would have a devotional meeting in the dining area where we had spiritual singing and an inspirational message by our minister, Rev. Eddie Randolph.

One evening before we were scheduled to leave we went to see the waterfall about ten miles from Chocola. We drove by the HTI Medical Clinic in a village near the waterfall. Dr. Castillo was very proud of the clinic made available to him by the HTI people.

On the way to the waterfall we could see banana trees everywhere with coffee plants underneath them.

To see the waterfall we had to walk about one-half mile from the road. It was such a quiet serene place, except for the water cascading 100 feet from above. The panoramic view was like a picture out of National Geographic. We all enjoyed the picturesque scenery to and from the waterfall. On our walk we saw men, women, and even some children carrying large loads of wood, mostly used for cooking. Some of these loads had to weigh over 150 pounds. "No wonder so many of the people here have hernias," I thought. On arriving back at the clinic area I saw one lady almost seventy years of age carrying on her head a tree trunk that would have tipped the scales at 100 pounds. Passing by were vehicles or "taxis", mostly trucks, loaded down with 15 to 20 people each.

The night before we left the local village church people held a celebration. A sermon was preached, songs sung, and then the children had fun breaking the pinata.

The gynecologists stopped operating two days before we left so they could discharge most or all of their patients on our departure day. The surgeons operated until the day before we left, as we sent most of the hernia repairs home the next day. All the patients that were left were cared for by Dr. Castillo and his group until well enough to be discharged.

Leaving was tearful for some of the team members. They had become good friends with the people who work there for HTI. After loading our bus we headed for Antigua, which was about a two-hour drive. Along the way we could see large fields of sugar cane, which was being harvested by hand but loaded mechanically onto trucks to take to the nearby mill. We saw neatly lined rows of planted rubber trees, many of which had tapping panels, a channel, and spout so the latex could drip into the collection cups.

We arrived in Antigua, a quaint old city with many narrow streets, on a warm but cloudy day. The city square was open and adorned with multiple businesses and the Catholic Church. Its facade must have been over a century old.

Everywhere women peddled their wares, especially the small colorful blankets. I purchased fourteen of these. Pastor Jerry Ervin, who had worked at the clinic starting IVs in the pre-surgery triage area—and who had become a good friend— was my guide and interpreter. He spoke excellent Spanish and had been there the previous year.

Jerry went with me into one of the nicer jewelry stores and looked at the jade necklaces, earrings, and bracelets. One of the salesmen recommended we go look at the jade factory down the street a few blocks, so we did with the salesman tagging along. Watching the multiple steps of jade jewelry being made from the rough to a finished product by cutting, grinding, and polishing it into beautiful product was fascinating. After touring the factory we went back to his store and I bought Vickie a gorgeous green-jade necklace.

The open-air market had many and various items, such as quilts, purses, jewelry of all types, clothes, and of course, blankets to buy. I continued to purchase a few other items when one young lady peddling the small colorful blankets approached me once again and said, "I have been following you all over town, and I'm so tired. Won't you buy one of my blankets now." And so I did.

A small group went with Vicki Ratts, R.N., to get some freshly ground coffee for gifts, souvenirs, and our own consumption. We were the last ones on the bus to proceed on to Guatemala City for the night.

The city was bustling with traffic as we went to our nice, modern hotel in Guatemala City. Finally utilizing the opportunity, I witnessed to my roommate who was not a professing Christian. He had told me he wanted to be a medical missionary in the future. I'm not sure of the outcome of this, but the seed was planted.

Early the next morning we climbed back on the bus and headed for the airport. Having spent all my money on the necklace and all the other goodies I had to borrow money from Carolyn to buy a Mundo Maya wall clock.

It was an excellent trip. We repaired nearly 60 hernias and the gynecologists did several hysterectomies and bladder repairs. The people we helped would never have been able to afford these procedures. The HTI organization made me feel part of it.

In February 2000 I went with the same group from Shreveport/Bossier City to Chocola, Guatemala. This year the surgeons were Grady Bruce, M.D., a urologist, Dr. Philip Strawther, M.D., a plastic surgeon, and me. Dr. Strawther performed several plastic surgeries.

One morning one of the local residents rushed to the clinic stating that his wife was having a very difficult time with labor and one of the baby's feet was protruding. The lady was rushed to the HTI clinic and delivered with the expertise of the OB-GYN doctors. I was doing a hernia repair during the delivery and missed some of the excitement. The delivery went well and mother and baby did fine.

Guatemala is an unusual place in that a lot of the hernias are femoral hernias. I got to do more femoral hernia repairs in five days than I had done in 29 years of operating back home.

At the end of the trip we went to Antigua for shopping. Again I bought more blankets and goodies.

In February 2001, Carolyn, Lynea, and Rod were not able to go, but I did. I felt so much a part of this group that I felt comfortable being with all the new people I got to meet on the trip. We went by the new location for the HTI clinic in Montellano which was several miles from Chocola. It was on a major highway and located on a beautiful site with a river nearby. Part of the walls were in place and construction was proceeding nicely.

In February 2002, Carolyn, Lynea, and I went on the inaugural trip to the new location for its dedication and first use. The Clinica Ezell has a surgery ward for 50 patients, 3 operating rooms, outpatient dispensary, pharmacy, kitchen and dining areas, and dormitories. These were now all complete, forming a beautiful complex. It was so nice! All this had been possible from gracious donors to the HTI. We felt honored to be the first to use the facility.

Also the new Montellano-San Miguel Church of Christ was ready and dedicated on Sunday. This too was a donated structure by the HTI organization.

The church and clinic were located very near a small river. Often we would walk by the river banks admiring its natural beauty. Women were doing their laundry in the river; children were swimming nearby; and further up the river men were fishing with nets and spears.

One day we rode to Chicacao as Montellano was just a small village. There we walked about the large city square and bought pastries to eat from one of the stores.

Two ophthalmologists were present on our trip, and they did several cataract surgeries. Dr. Strawther was back and he did more plastic surgeries. We general surgeons did a lot of hernia repairs. The gynecological surgeons did a lot of hysterectomies.

We made our annual trip to Antigua also.

In April 2003 I returned to the Clinica Ezell with Carolyn and Lynea. The hospital grounds had its landscaping completed now. It was just an oasis in the middle of a jungle. Zack, the HTI intern, from the previous year had become engaged to one of the local Guatemala women; she had the classical beauty of a Mayan princess.

Dr. Bruce did the first prostatectomy at the HTI clinics. Dr. Enrique Duprat, general surgeon, and his wife became good friends of mine. We would go over to Dr. Sergio Castillo's new home on the complex and watch the Iraq War news on CNN.

The general surgeons did a near record number of hernia repairs for the week. The gynecological surgeons did many vaginal hysterectomies. Dr. Bruce helped them with some of the complicated bladder repairs.

Most of us loaded up in the trucks and went back to the waterfalls past Chocola, then came back by the old HTI clinic in Chocola. It was sad to see how it was deteriorating without HTI occupying it.

We made our Antigua trip again and stayed overnight in Guatemala City prior to departing the next day.

I praise HTI for its evangelical work through the churches and for its medical and surgical work preformed for the indigent of that area who could not afford it. I always considered the trip there a blessing to me—from the appreciation of the people there and the friendly people with whom I worked.

CHAPTER 7

Trip to Mexico with LSU Students

March 1999

In December 1998 during Lottie Moon Christmas Offering month Charles Walker, Th.D., director of Baptist Student Union at LSU Medical School in Shreveport, was invited to our church, Airline Baptist Church in Bossier City, to give a message on missions. He gave a very interesting talk about his recent trip to Cuba and trying to set up mission work there.

At the end of the message, I had a personal talk with him about future mission trips. Dr. Walker informed me that he was going on a trip with a rather large group of medical students to Piedgras Negras in northern Mexico in March 1999. I told him I would be interested in going, but he already had five physicians who had volunteered to go. I asked him to let me know if any openings became available.

Two months later Dr. Walker called and told me all the other physicians had dropped out for one reason or the other. He wanted to know if I would consider going. I told him I would. About one week prior to leaving for Mexico we met at the Parkview Baptist Church in Shreveport and packed supplies, medications, and gear for our trip. During that time a reporter from *The Shreveport Times* interviewed several of the students. He also asked me about the trip. I told him that I

51

planned to do more and more of these trips in the future.

The last week in March 1999, during Easter break for the LSU Med School, Dr. Walker, Skip Noble, Baptist Student Union Director at the LSU's campus, and I each drove a van from Shreveport through San Antonio, Texas to Eagle Pass. We crossed the border by going over the Rio Grande River into Piedgras Negras (an industrial city just south of the border). Twenty-six freshman and sophomore LSU med students along with a few others were on the trip. We drove into the city to find a missionary compound owned and run by Dr. Juarez, M.D. This compound had dormitory facilities, kitchen, dining area, and classrooms for missionary and evangelical groups. We had grocery shopped in Eagle Pass since we knew we would be preparing our own meals. A volunteer group cooked breakfast and supper every day and a detail cleaned up after meals.

The next day being Sunday we all went to church at Gigal Baptist Church where Dr. Juarez was the pastor. We found out he also pastored a couple of other outlying smaller churches on Sundays. He does a lot of local mission work and has two locations where young children can eat free, if their parents consent to attending church on Sunday. He started this ministry about three years earlier at one site. It was very successful in helping the nutrition of the children and getting adults into church, and it had grown to two sites, and a third was being planned. We had talent with us so we got to sing in the church and one of the students played his guitar.

Early Monday morning our group divided into three teams—two teams that would go to local churches in the area to do medical clinics while a third team worked on clearing where the newly purchased site for a new church and medical clinic were to be built in the near future.

A group of freshman med students went with me daily.

Together we would evaluate patients, discuss their problem(s), and medicate or treat them as indicated. Other students staffed our pharmacy with medicines that Dr. Walker had obtained from CrossLinks International. Dr. Juarez said this was a good way to get people familiar with and involved in the churches with whom we were ministering. Since we were exposed to a foreign language, this turned out to be an excellent opportunity to learn a little Spanish. Susan, who had taken Spanish in high school, quickly recalled her Spanish and was interpreting and speaking fluently in the language by the end of the week.

The other medical team of sophomore students was assigned to Michael Willmore, a physician assistant. The week went by rapidly and the students were a joy to work with. The people were always friendly and on more than one occasion we ate lunch at one of the local pastors' homes and enjoyed some real home-cooked Mexican food. We got to see the industrial city of Piedgras Negras where many of the homes were very nice, but on the other side of the tracks we saw marked poverty with people living in cardboard houses or shanty towns. Dr. Walker called this the feminization of poverty because so many mothers with children were in the poverty group.

We celebrated the last night by eating a big steak dinner at the mission house. I could tell the students appreciated me as I had tried to teach and train as we endeavored together. The following day we drove back to Shreveport in our vans.

I learned to appreciate Dr. Charles Walker's efforts to get the medical students interested in mission work at this early stage of their training. This exposure to missions is an excellent way to draw one to the mission field. God may call some of these students to a life of mission work as career missionaries. This trip further convinced me that my future lay in this type of ministry.

CHAPTER 8

The Land of the Safari Kenya

July 24-August 5, 1999

In late June 1999 Dr. Charles Walker called again about another mission trip. He said he initially had about two dozen doctors interested in a medical-mission trip to Embu, Kenya, in late July, early August. He had set up the medical part with IMB missionaries Jo and Louie Scales. But from all the Shreveport First Baptist doctors, only one doctor signed up to go. Charles wanted to know if I would go. I told him that I would if my wife, Vickie, could go. He readily agreed.

Vickie and I met all the participants during our preliminary and preparatory meetings at the First Baptist Church in Shreveport. Dr. Bill Pate (otolaryngologist) was the other doctor. His wife, Vicky, accompanied him. Vickie and I took an instant liking to Dr. Jon Stubblefield, pastor of First Baptist Church in Shreveport, and his wife, Jackie. First Baptist Church of Shreveport had been chosen to host the annual missionary retreat and Vacation Bible School at Brackenhurst Retreat Center. All the IMB missionaries in Africa and their children that could were expected there. Initially it was just the retreat, but Dr. Walker got permission and set up the medical team to go to Embu with the Scales. The medical team would leave first. Then the evangelical or retreat team would join them about the time we were leaving; some of the medical team would accompany the retreat team.

Betty Ann McQueen, retired IMB missionary to Nigeria for almost 30 years, was to head up our evangelistic (spiritual) station in the medical clinic. We likewise had an instant bonding with her because of her spiritual mannerism. The Rev. Mel Brown was to head up the pastoral team. He was a pastor from a local church in Shreveport. Our medical group had to go without Dr. Walker as he had just started his physician-assistant program at LSU Medical School in Shreveport.

The medical team flew from Shreveport through Memphis to Amsterdam. A few hours later we were on the way to Kenya in the most cramped space I've ever experienced on the Kenya Airlines. We arrived in Nairobi the next morning and met Dr. Glen Smith, career IMB missionary to Kenya, at the airport. We loaded our luggage and supplies and proceeded toward Embu, approximately 90 miles northeast of Nairobi. Along the way we saw several open markets on the outskirts of Nairobi, the capital city of Kenya. Looking back on the city from near the municipal limits we could tell it was a large city with only a few tall buildings. Occasionally we would see a high-rise apartment building with laundry hanging on the porches to dry.

Mount Kilamanjaro stood in the distance, but due to the haze we could not really make out any details. We were told that on a clear day you could easily see the snow-capped peak.

Several miles from Nairobi we stopped at Thika Falls, a small beautiful resort to relax a moment and refreshen with a cup of hot tea or coffee. Outside was a waterfall and a garden that was adorned with flowering trees and shrubs. We proceeded toward Embu and noticed the small hills with sparse bushes, a few trees, and minimal grass. This was the dry season for Kenya. The country had been experiencing a drought for several months. Occasionally when the hills vanished and flat land took its place we saw a few rice fields.

Finally we arrived at the Isaak Walton Inn, built in 1943, but the nicest Embu had to offer. The hotel was surrounded by well proportioned pretty shrubs, plants, and flowers. The rooms were very ample. There was no fan or air conditioning, as we were over 5,000-feet above sea level. Embu is in the southern hemisphere where it was winter in July and August. There we met Jo and Louie Scales, the host missionaries with whom we were to work. They were happy to see us. Jo and Louie loved the Kenyan people and after almost thirty years of service there they had at one time thought about staying there in retirement; one of their friends had recently done just that.

That night at supper we met our interpreters so they could get use to our Southern accents. They too had a strange accents to us. Later that evening we finished dose packing the meds for the clinic the next day.

The following morning we loaded all our meds and supplies and headed out of town past the open market to Karurina Baptist Church. The church was set off a dirt road in a cornfield but nicely constructed of cinder blocks. Some people had already arrived and many more followed expecting free medical treatment. The people were very colorfully dressed in their Sunday best with 3 or 4 layers; it was 60 to 65 degrees in the cool and crisp air.

Triage was set up at the front entrance to the church. Dr. Bill Pate and I staffed the medical stations on either side of the church walls. Then people next went to our pharmacy and finally to the most important station, the spiritual station with Betty McQueen and occasionally Dr. Smith. With the aid of interpreters we saw many people with multiple maladies and treated them the best we could. We would occasionally consult

Dr. Smith for the more unusual or complicated cases. We saw several children with the usual winter colds.

Rev. Mel Brown gave morning sermons each day and gathered with all the pastors that came to our clinics in the churches. The people listened intently to his message of Jesus and His saving grace.

The weather remained cool in the morning and very pleasant in the evening with a slight haze but few clouds. This was late winter in this part of Kenya. The atmosphere was ideal for a missionary effort.

We visited the Itabua Baptist Church the following day. It had a nice cinder-block building. We were greeted by a small crowd, but the lines lengthened and seemed endless by the time Jo had set for us to leave. Dr. Pate and I saw many of the usual maladies that most people have, but we also treated some of the local illnesses such as malaria, which was different to us. Nutrition, pain from working all day every day, and skin disorders seemed to be the most common things we saw and treated. Jo told the crowd that remained to come down the road to where we would hold our clinic the next day. It was only a short walk. The people were very gracious and didn't seem to mind.

Rianjeru Baptist Church was our next stop the following day. It was built from rough, native-made lumber and had a dirt floor. I got ill that day as I had eaten a can of tuna fish we had brought from home. A few times between patients I vomited in a plastic sack. At other times while seeing a patient I would excuse myself and vomit right in front of the patient and continue on as if nothing had ever happened. They acted as if this was a thing I did on a regular basis. Jo wanted to take me back to the hotel, but I told her I was fine as long as I was busy. The people were so gracious and grateful that we had come their way. Many of these people had never before seen a doctor.

Thursday night we went over to the Scales home which was surrounded by a wall, had steel bars on the windows, and a guard 24 hours a day because of thievery. Louie and Jo cooked hamburgers, which was a break from the soul food we had been eating at the hotel restaurant. I finally got into a private conversation with Jo and she told me the story of why she and Louie became foreign missionaries. She told me that a young age she had dedicated herself to becoming a foreign missionary and never forgot that promise she had made to God. She met Louie and had fallen in love with him, but did not consent to marry him until one night when they were at a revival and he dedicated himself to foreign missions—a match in heaven had been made. They had been in Kenya for almost 30 years.

The Gatumbiri Baptist Church was a wood-frame structure with mud walls. We had been seeing patients all morning. Then at noon the nearby local school let out so the children could come see medical missionaries from the US. There must have been over 200 children from ages 6 to 12. One of the school teachers said it was a miracle from God that our medical team had come, since most of them had never seen a doctor before. We really saw a lot of skin disorders and lesions such as ringworm and sores caused by lack of hygiene because water for bathing was almost unheard of; the mother or females in the household would have to walk 4 to 8 miles just to get drinking water.

Friday afternoon, July 30, 1999, after clinic Dr. Pate wanted to go to the Embu Provincial Hospital which was just down the road from our hotel, so Vickie, Vicky, and I went along too. After introducing ourselves to the administrative office we were welcomed by the hospital administrator; he was an oncologist physician. He graciously showed us around the hospital grounds which had bright-colored flowers everywhere. As we were touring the hospital which was a series of masonry houses, we went by the only operating room. A surgery crew was starting to operate on a baby with an incarcerated inguinal hernia. I volunteered to help, but the procedure was underway. The administrator explained that of the 18,000 patients seen yearly in the clinics there, 1,800 were admitted and nearly 70% of these had AIDS. The doctors only could treat them symptomatically because the anti-virals required to treat AIDS were too expensive for the hospital's budget. We toured two wards of AIDS patients and saw patients in all stages of the fatal disease.

The last day of clinics we went to Kiritiri Baptist Church and saw as many patients as we could. The nurses and other personnel went outside and treated wounds and burns while we labored inside. Jo always had us stop at a reasonable time as the sun set about 6 p.m. on the equator. She also did not want to completely wear out her medical help. Our interpreters were a valuable asset; they tried so hard to help as well as to interpret for us. My interpreter was a joy to work with.

We toured the Kamburu Dam down the road, but no water was flowing over the spillway because of the drought conditions that had prevailed for some time.

Sunday morning we heard Rev. Mel Brown preach in English; it was translated to Swahili by Louie. The choir was the most rhythmic and enthusiastic I have seen anywhere. The drums and triangles just added to the atmosphere. Young children danced in front of the choir. The service was very memorable.

Sunday afternoon we rode around in vans to see the countryside. We went to see Runyenges Baptist Church. The Scales had bought the church's land and paid a good portion of the construction costs for its building; The building itself was built by summer mission-church builders. The Scales were very proud of this church for the local people they loved so much.

Tea fields dotted the horizon. These replaced the coffee fields as tea was more profitable, according to Louie. Along the small river down from a nearby waterfall vegetables, maze, and banana trees were cultivated because of the available water there. In contrast, the surrounding fields reflected the effect of the dry season and drought.

Our group drove back to Nairobi the following day. During this journey Louie showed us where he and Jo had been ambushed and robbed; Jo was shot twice in her leg near her pelvis. Louie did not stop, rather he ran through their blockade and rushed her to the hospital in Nairobi where it took some time to recover. This did not deter their love and mission for the country of Kenya. We spent the night in Nairobi in a nice hotel.

The following day we went to the Nairobi National Park (Kifaru Ark or Rhino Sanctuary). We went on a brief safari out onto the serengetti and saw many zebras, wildebeests, giraffes, elands, and only an occasional hippopotamus before coming to the majestic lions. Our vehicle allowed us to come within six feet of the male lion who had many scars from the fighting off younger males competing for his pride of nine lionesses and many cubs. We saw two white rhinoceri at a distance. Their numbers were small because of all the poachers who had decimated their numbers. Now armed guards on duty twenty-four hours a day in the park protect them. Then we saw a male ostrich chasing his female counterpart across the plain at speeds near 50 miles per hour, only to change directions in a flash, and then disappear behind a clump of bushes.

Continuing with the unusual, we went to the Carnivore Restaurant and ate for lunch home-grown ostrich, eland, impala, giraffe, crocodile, and zebra. Then we proceeded to the petting zoo where the missionary retreat and Vacation Bible School teams caught up with us; they were dragging from fatigue and jet lag from almost two days of travel.

The night before we parted we had a banquet with both the medical and retreat teams and all the missionaries at our hotel. It was a delight to hear the testimonies of how all the members of the medical team had enjoyed the trip and what a blessing it had meant to them. The missionaries were encouraged by our visit and so grateful. The Scales, Dr. Smith and his entire family were there.

It seemed difficult to really show our appreciation for their gracious and kind efforts during the mission trip.

We felt the trip to be a huge success. The medical team had seen over 600 people; its spiritual station had led several dozen to accept Jesus as Lord and Savior. This would help build the churches with whom we had worked.

I heard later that the missionary retreat and Vacation Bible School at the Brackenhurst Retreat Center had been a great success also. All available African IMB missionaries and their families had come for the week-long retreat. Vacation Bible School was held for the missionary children.

From the trip I learned the basic format of the different stations and the most important, the spiritual station. The career missionaries really had been educational, inspirational, and motivational.

Our team then flew back to Amsterdam where we spent several hours there touring the city, including Anne Frank's House. We even went shopping for a spell at one of the malls.

I agreed with Vickie when she said we really enjoyed this trip.

Chapter 9

Retirement from Private Practice

September 1999

    For years I had dreamed of retiring one day and depend on the stock market for satisfactory income. In the 1990s I had done quite well with my investments. Then came 2000.

    I was blessed with a hospital staff that was friendly and always helpful, especially when I consulted the other doctors to help with my patients' medical or surgical problem(s). Most of my patients came from the city and parish, but many came from as far away as 60-plus miles. After getting started, I never lacked for a number of patients until I fired all the HMOs (Health Management Organizations).

    I came into town quietly and probably left the quietest of anyone ever. A new administration had just taken over Bossier Medical Center the previous month. No retirement party was ever mentioned. I thought at least I would get a vaginal speculum like Dr. C.H. McCuller did when he retired; he had complained that he had been charged for one of those when he was hospitalized the year before; so at his retirement party, he finally got one as a gag gift.

    I felt blessed to have earned a nice living even though the work days were often 14 to 16 hours. I gave up a lot of time from my wife and children to nurture my practice, but it was extremely rewarding over the years. I can't go to the mall, Wal-Mart, Albertsons, or a restaurant in town that I don't see some of my former patients who state that they really miss me and wish I was back in practice. I tell them that I felt like the last Mohican of solo practice, like the old family doctor when I decided to retire from practice. I had tried on a few occasions to get a partner, but it never panned out.

Many reasons culminated in my decision to finally retire from private practice; I will try to elaborate on a few of them. My main reason was the promise I had made to God in Israel in December 1998 to do the Great Commission. In February 1999 I had started doing short-term mission trips and loved the pleasure of taking the Gospel to various countries and the excitement of traveling to all corners of the world. The more trips I went on, the more I got into it. My calling was calling me.

In November of 1998 I had decided to drop general surgery and do just general or family practice for two or three years. The malpractice premiums had escalated over the years to the point that if I dropped from a Class V risk to a Class I risk the malpractice insurance would be minimal instead of large for the three years. (I didn't know at the time that the Louisiana Medical Mutual Insurance Company did not require you pay a tail if you were a charter member like me.)

Over the years I had built a large practice by being available. During my 25 years in solo practice—having sufficient ability and ample affability—I tried to be personal with all my patients. I returned all calls as soon as possible. I even called the lab and/or x-ray department to discuss their results and determine if further diagnosis or treatment was needed. If you are familiar with your doctor now, you may know that this is a luxury most physicians don't provide these days. I was spending two to three hours a day on the phone, particularly calling in prescriptions or refills. To be honest it almost got aggravating to have to treat some of my patients over the phone and then call them in a prescription too.

Also along came a few malpractice cases. Most of these were dropped, but finally I had one which essentially broke my back. That case was later dropped by the patient when she understood why all that happened had occurred.

But I guess the most aggravating thing of all was "mangled medicine" brought on by managed care. The insurance companies controlled a lot of the medical care you could provide—and often paid you less and less, if at all. As an example: I was called at 5 p.m. on a Friday, just before leaving my office, by the Emergency Room for a patient with possible acute appendicitis. I promptly went to the Emergency Room, examined the patient, took him to the operating room, and had completed an appendectomy all within the scope of one and one-half hours. Then I discharged him doing well within 24 hours. I had tried to call the HMO, but it was after 5 p.m. on Friday. When I called on Monday and told HMO personnel I had operated on the patient without their approval on Friday, they would not approve payment—and they didn't, even when I took it all the way to the state level.

Another factor was near burnout. I had found a new love: mission work. The daily ongoing practice was getting to be unsatisfying. One day a young man came in demanding I give him some Lortab. I told him he had no reason for any, but he demanded over and over emphatically that I give him a prescription for this drug. Finally I mumbled under my breath that he was acting like an "_ _ _ hole". He apparently heard me and asked if I was calling him an "_ _ _hole". I told him to take the anti-inflammatories I had given him and leave. The patient left cursing, not knowing all this was heard by my wife who was working as my receptionists at the time. She reminded him that he was talking much worse than he claimed I did. I called his grandparents, with whom he was living, and told them of the situation. They thought nothing of it, but I did. I knew then that it was getting time to act on the thought of retiring from private practice.

The final straw that broke the camel's back was income. I had finally fired all the HMOs, thinking my patients would stick with me. They did as long as they could. Finally my wife and I realized we were working for expenses only, so it was time to pursue other alternatives and do what I really wanted to do: mission work.

I took the ACLS (Advanced Cardiac Life Support) course the day before I retired from private practice and was to start work in the Bossier Medical Center Emergency Room the day after my retirement. All Emergency Rooms require their workers to take the ACLS course.

The last day in private practice was quite memorable. That day was one of my busiest ever; I had placed an advertisement in the paper and many of my patients wanted to see me one last time, mostly to stock up on medications, until they could find a new practicing doctor. It just turned out that my last patient (Cooksey Humphrey) was the son of my first patient in private practice (Louis Humphrey). I knew then that a generation had truly passed!

Chapter 10

The Siam Experience Thailand

November 1999

    Major events had already occurred in readying me for retirement from private practice and "halftime". I had just formally retired from private practice after almost 25 years and was to start working part time in the Emergency Room at Bossier Medical Center the day after I retired. But five hours before I was to start work there, I was informed that I would not be needed after all. What a let down. Also I was making arrangements to sell my office.
    After returning from the Mexico trip, Dr. Charles Walker told me to contact Dr. James Williams of the Baptist Medical Dental Fellowship in Memphis if I wanted to pursue short-term medical-mission trips. When I called, I was pleasantly greeted and welcomed to any help with opportunities for short-term mission work.
    I had just obtained a computer so that I could do medical-mission work, and Jim (Dr. James Williams) emailed me two missionaries' email addresses. One of these was Dr. John Gibson in Nan; I thought this was in China as I had told Jim I was interested in going to China. After emailing John (Dr. Gibson) and telling of my interests in doing medical missions,

I received a response back informing me that he was located in north Thailand serving the hill tribes there just south of Laos.

Apparently Dr. Gibson informed the people in Gainesville, Florida, that I was interested in going to Nan as they had been scheduled to visit there soon. Two days later I received an email from the Westside Baptist Church in Gainesville, Florida, stating that they needed a doctor or two and team members for a trip to north Thailand. I responded and got the telephone number of Sandra Benton, R.N., whom I called and found out that she had a team ready to go to Thailand, but for one reason or the other it had dissipated. I told her I could get a team together if she would coordinate the trip; she agreed.

During the next two weeks I invited several dozen people to go on the mission trip with us. Of those I had recruited two retired nurses (Rose Mary Andrews and Joyce Keith), a lay minister (Cullen Keith), a dentist (Dr. Roger Arnold), my wife (Vickie), one of my Sunday School Department members (Joyce Evans), and one of my patients (Monica Wolfe).

Although a little on the expensive side, I called Dr. Gibson twice and got an idea of what to bring. I gathered all the samples and medical supplies left over from my recent practice. Soon we were ready to travel.

We were to meet Sandra Benton and Al George in Los Angeles. Weather problems between Florida and Los Angeles nixed that plan, so Sandra and Al had to go literally the opposite direction—via Paris, France, to get to Bangkok. Our group flew to Los Angeles, then through Sappiro, Japan, to Bangkok where we all met. After that long tiring flight, we all checked into a hotel for the remainder of the night. The next morning we flew to Chang Mai, then on to Nan where we met our transfer team that would take us on to the Gibsons.

We were taken several miles north of Nan to the Gibsons'

compound known as Chiangklank Baptist Clinic. This consisted of a large clinic, a house with three sets of rooms equivalent to 3 homes, and a dormitory that would house at least 20 people. John later told us that a very dear friend who wanted to be a missionary, but couldn't because of family situations, donated most of the money to build this beautiful complex.

We then met Linda Gibson and their three daughters. We proceeded on to the clinic to meet Dr. John Gibson, who was busy seeing patients. Here John would see tribal and northern Thai patients. After a brief tour of the clinic, he put me to work excising a cyst from one of the patient's lips and Dr. Arnold to work pulling teeth. Later we unloaded all our supplies and meds to get ready for the clinic he had planned the next day, but he already had prepacked supplies for the first clinic.

The next morning, after a much-needed night of rest we loaded up and traveled by pickup trucks to Nam Gee to set up a clinic. Many of the people turned out in their native clothes of the Mienh. They were quite colorful in what we would almost call a costume with knitted red hats and head wear. Dr. Gibson had made a large sign announcing the clinic with free medical and dental care. Rhonda, a career IMB missionary and dentist, joined us later and helped in the clinic.

Many routine maladies were often seen and treated. All too often we saw large goiters resulting from low iodine in their diet. We also saw a few older men who appeared emaciated. Dr. Gibson told us that they were addicted to opium. That evening we got to explore the village and saw women in their yards under a shade tree crocheting, men threshing rice, and livestock everywhere. The people were very friendly and welcomed our brief exploration of their habitat.

That evening we shared the Gospel with messages and

movies. To show the movie a big white sheet was strung up across part of a soccer field in front of the local school. A large crowd showed up and stayed until we closed the service. It is by this means of ministering to the people there that Christian churches can be built and those already there can be strengthened. John and Linda do these mobile clinics often, especially when short-term mission groups are available to help. We spent the night in our small tents inside the local school to avoid mosquitoes. We had the luxury of a cook accompanying us to prepare our meals. We spent two days at the clinic ministering to the people.

Early Sunday morning we journeyed to the church at the New Vision Dorm operated by the Persets. We attended the church service with all the children and workers that morning. Vickie got to play her flute. Cullen Keith gave an inspiring message that included salvation through Jesus. Thirty-four of the children accepted Jesus; these were later counseled by Al George to make sure of their decisions. We then toured the whole facility including the dorm rooms, cafeteria, and a parcel of land down by a stream where much of their fruit and vegetables were grown for the orphanage.

We ate lunch in Nan, spent the night at the Gibson compound, and got ready for the clinic the next day at Way du Lang. Dr. Gibson was busy in the Chiangklang Clinic so Dr. Mac, a native of Scotland, went to help at our clinic. We stayed again in tents at a local school. The following day we worked from 8 a.m. to 8:30 p.m. seeing almost 500 people. That night we showed films and held a service for the people.

The following day we went by a shop where jewelry, ornaments, and all types of things were being made from silver. Linda found out some folks were having a wedding just up the hill. We were invited to visit as one of our team workers was related to the bride.

The atmosphere was festive as we approached the wedding party. We were invited to sit and have punch. The costumes and native clothes were extremely colorful. The bride and groom (17 and 18 years of age) were adorned in headdress and colorful clothes with multiple silver ornaments, the type you see in *National Geographic* magazines.

The cousin of the bride, who had been working with us in the clinics, had heard Vickie play her flute. She asked her if she would play at the wedding. Vickie played *I Love Thee*, a good Christian song in a Buddhist wedding. The bride personally thanked her before we left.

On the way back to the Gibson compound, we stopped at a small waterfall which was very picturesque. We then had a day of rest. I read almost the entire book *Fresh Wind, Fresh Fire* by Jim Cymbala. At one point, Vickie wanted to know why tears were flowing down my face. I told her to just wait until she read the book. We went to a loom-silk-weaving factory and later to an outlet store where the girls bought some silk cloth to make dresses.

When we arrived back at the compound, a rainbow was adorning the sky across the western sky. The cultivated fields of rice and different crops in this panorama made the countryside look so peaceful. In the distance was a large Buddhist temple.

That night we celebrated Katie Gibson's birthday. We gave the Gibsons a few presents we had brought. The next morning we loaded up again for our last clinic at Bang Kaa. Dr. Arnold decided he had to leave early and proceeded to Bangkok before he went back home.

We journeyed to Bang Kaa and set up clinic in the Civic Center. We had a clinic that afternoon and had a worship service that night and showed films. We set up our tents in the

Civic Center and spent the night so we could hold clinic again the next day.

The following day was Sunday so we traveled to minister to the Hmong people at Whay Juke, just a few miles below the Laos border. Linda told us that over the mountain range there were no IMB missionaries. She said they had been praying for someone to volunteer to go to south Laos.

We held church in a local home where we sang and three of us gave testimonies. I told them of our trip to the Holy Land earlier that year. The Christians there, although small in number, were very faithful even though they had been ostracized by the local Buddhists. They were now considered dead people. The Buddhist monks no longer gave them fertilizer to help with their rice crops. According to Linda, the people were no longer spoken to or socialized with; they had been taunted and ridiculed. These simple rice farmers however had found the real truth—they had found Jesus and seemed proud of that. I felt gratitude toward these people who had basically given up a way of life to worship the true, living God. If only some of the people back home could see faith in action like this small group of people, now isolated from their world because of their beliefs. Their reward one day will be given by the One they worship.

We enjoyed helping the Gibsons with their ministry to the hill tribes of north Thailand, mainly the Mienh and Hmong peoples. John and Linda witness daily in the clinic at Chiangklang Baptist Clinic where they work, and as often as possible in field trips to the other people in the countryside.

We left Nan and flew to Chang Mai where we found a Kentucky Fried Chicken restaurant; we were so happy to have American food again instead of rice twice daily. We loved shopping for souvenirs at night along the main street. The following morning we went to the Mesa Elephant Camp and saw elephants up close, petted some of them, and even rode some big ones in a carriage on top. Then we got to see an elephant talent show. It was amazing how the elephants could dance, walk on two back legs, and even kick a soccer ball over 120 feet.

Next door was an orchid nursery that we toured and where we saw some of the most beautiful plants that we had ever seen.

The next morning we flew back to Bangkok. That evening some of us rented a motorized rickshaw (most popular form of transportation) and went out to a carving shop where world renown (registered) carvings of elephants are made. We purchased one, which was so realistic.

The next day we went to the Grand Palace, which is a large Buddhist Compound with huge pagodas, some of which were gold plated. The palace is at least six square blocks in size. The temple of the Green Emerald Buddha was the big attraction.

The next day we flew back the long way home. It was a very good trip, but personalities do arise, and adjustments have to be made. The Gibsons were very appreciative of our help in their ministry to the hill tribes of north Thailand.

Chapter 11

Halftime

The definite metamorphosis of "halftime" for me started in October of 1998. I had decided to start winding down from private practice. I dropped my general-surgery privileges at all the local hospitals where I had staff privileges and changed them to general practice status. My idea was to cut the cost of malpractice insurance by 70% with less risk status, and a three year tail was required.

Immediately I felt a big difference in work load, patients, and income, but I missed my privileges as a surgeon the most.

The HMO's were a continuing source of aggravation so I decided to fire them all. I kept busy for several months, but as time went by my patients, who had been loyal for years, had to follow their insurance plans. I could understand that. The process of treating over the telephone got worse, but I tried to help out as much as I could. It seems I was spending as much as two to three hours per day on the telephone. I tried sharing calls with one or two of the family practitioners, but that too was often one sided. To some of my favorite patients I kidded them that I was going to join the Diesel Driving Academy for a change of pace.

Vickie and I went to Israel in late December 1998 and there I had that encounter where I promised God that I would serve him by doing the Great Commission.

Actually my mind was made up, but I lingered on until the

economics of practice, especially with the deletion of several insurance groups, made it obvious that it was time to move on.

Our trip to Kenya and Thailand had already been planned. The term Halftime came along just as we were packing for Kenya. This process of going from success to significance had begun. I actually retired from private practice just before going to Thailand. The letdown of the job I had lined up in the Bossier Medical Center Emergency Room was indeed a big letdown; I had planned on working just enough for expenses and have a lot of time to go on short-term, medical-mission trips.

Finally the reality of retirement began to sink in. I missed seeing all my patients; I missed all the camaraderie of my fellow physicians, and I missed the income from my practice.

Frankly I became depressed. I began to withdraw for a while and was even questioning my decision to retire. Then one day I visited one of my friends in the hospital, Rev. Billy Pierce, and related to him my plans for the future. He told me that I needed training in evangelism, if I was making that my priority in life. Having taken the course himself at Broadmoor Baptist Church in Shreveport, he told me that I should take the F.A.I.T.H. course that had been started by Rev. Bobby Welch, Doug Williams, and David Apple in Daytona Beach, Florida. He told me of the results of this at his church. He said it was a significant way to introduce the Gospel to many people. He told me if I had to fly out of state to take it to do so. He asked if I would call Dr. Larry Williams at Broadmoor and ask when the next course was to be offered. That was on a Thursday, and a new session of the F.A.I.T.H. program just happened to be starting that Sunday afternoon. Larry gave me a special invitation to join them, and I readily accepted.

The F.A.I.T.H. course lasted for 16 weeks; the training sessions were on Sunday afternoons, and the visitations were on Tuesday nights. Dr. Williams (Larry) and the group made me feel so at home that I felt I was part of their church. It was a most valuable course. On our fourth trip out on visitation a fourteen-year-old girl accepted Jesus as her Lord and Savior.

Meanwhile, I frequently read some great religious books. I read *Experiencing God* by Henry Blackaby and spent four to five hours daily on the accompanying workbook course. The *Experiencing God* book and course actually made me forget about my depression. The experience pointed me toward the purpose I had wanted all along. Truly the Holy Bible had spoken to me through Isaiah 40:31:

But they that wait upon the Lord shall renew their strength, they shall mount up with wings as eagles, they shall run and not be weary; and they shall walk and not faint. I felt energized.

The stock market was going south and my ready cash reserves began to deplete, so I sought part-time work in an emergency room elsewhere. I called my long-standing friend and old roommate, Dr. James Hudson, in Minden and after a few forms and formalities from an emergency-room agency I was working again, although only once or twice a week. Meanwhile, I continued the F.A.I.T.H. course and continued reading several more religious books.

When I went to Winnfield to work at the Winn Parish Medical Center Emergency Room the nurses asked who I was. I proceeded to tell them I was a Great-Commission Christian taking the F.A.I.T.H. course and asked if I could practice on them with the F.A.I.T.H. presentation. No one seemed very interested until a few minutes later as I was walking back to my room. The emergency-room clerk approached me and told me that her husband was a good man but not a Christian. She asked if I would give him the F.A.I.T.H. presentation soon. I volunteered to do so the next shift I worked there in three days. She said he didn't get off work until 11 p.m., so I asked them to meet me at midnight in my room down from the nurses station.

I prayed and prepared the best presentation I had done to date. I think the man and his wife must have both been praying also. They attentively listened as I calmly gave the presentation. Jason accepted the Lord as Savior and two weeks later on Easter Sunday was baptized into their church as a new Christian.

Our second trip to Israel was approaching. We left on schedule for Israel, but I missed my graduation from F.A.I.T.H. I later received my F.A.I.T.H. pin to proudly display on my coat lapel.

Meanwhile, I had gotten more proficient at the F.A.I.T.H. course. I remembered three weeks after I had started the course fumbling through the presentation to a young Thai girl (Pin, short for Saipin Kanganavasa) who had flown to the U.S. for some major dental procedures. Pin and Dr. Roger Arnold, who had gone with us to Thailand on our recent medical mission trip, had been in a major head-on motor-vehicle accident. He had suffered pelvic and leg fractures and was recuperating at Lagniappe Hospital. When I visited, Pin was reading a Bible. I asked if she was a Christian. She stated that she was considering it, so I gave the F.A.I.T.H. presentation the best I could, but she was not convinced. I got my second chance several weeks later when I invited myself over to Dr. Arnold's home; he was still walking with a walker. I asked Pin if I could present the F.A.I.T.H. presentation to her again. She agreed, so she and I went to the kitchen table and with the properly given F.A.I.T.H. presentation she accepted Jesus as

Savior. She related to me that she was leaving to go back to Thailand in two weeks and that she wanted to be baptized in my church before she left. I talked with my pastor, Dr. Damon Vaughn, and he agreed to baptize her. I was flying out of Shreveport that morning to Benin, Africa, on another medical mission trip, so I missed her baptism.

A month later I received a postcard from Saipin Kanganavasa (Pin) stating that she had joined a Baptist church just outside Bangkok and was attending regularly. She said she was trying to witness to her Buddhist family to become Christians.

Thanks to evangelical training with the F.A.I.T.H. course, taking the *Experiencing God* workbook course, reading multiple religious books, praying every day at devotion time, and working part time in various emergency rooms, I felt ready to proceed to the second half of my life.

CHAPTER 12

Return to the Holy Land Commissioning for My Work
May 2000

Having enjoyed so much the Holy Land tour in December 1998 though January 1999, Vickie and I decided to go again with Rev. Mike Gilcrease. My incentive was a little different this time. In December 1998 I had promised God I would commit my life to the Great Commission. Now I wanted to return and as a commissioning service be baptized in the Jordan River.

Mike had encouraged me to invite several people on this trip so I could get "free trips" for every sixth person invited. Using one of my other talents, I was able to recruit ten people so Dr. Damon V. Vaughn and his wife, Carolyn, could go with us. My plan was to have my pastor, Dr. Vaughn, go so he could baptize me in the Jordan River. I felt this would be an appropriate commissioning to the service I promised. This time we chose to go on the extra trip to the Greek Isles scheduled after Israel.

The different groups of our total entourage met at JFK Airport in New York City, went to La Guardia Airport, then flew to Athens, where we toured the city for a day. It was so nice to have Donnie Gilcrease along this time; she was recovering from recent chemotherapy. Also Charles and Gayle Laughridge were there again.

Traveling by bus we made our way to the Acropolis and Parthenon. As he had done on a previous trip, Dr. Vaughn preached on Mars Hill about Paul and his sermon on Mars Hill. On the way to the Acropolis, we went by the old amphitheater, then on to the Parthenon. It was interesting to see the original Parthenon and surrounding structures, as this type architecture had been copied so many times in the U.S. It was a beautiful sunny day, but the brisk wind with gusts up to 40 miles per hour sent chills into us. While there, we visited the museum adjacent to the Parthenon, then proceeded back to our hotel.

The next day we flew to Tel Aviv and spent the night before starting the Holy Land tour.

The ruins in Jaffa were very interesting. We saw statue images reminding us of Abraham's intended sacrifice of Isaac. We found out that the Promised Land "flowing with milk and honey" was actually fig (white juice of the fig—called milk) and honey (actually dates; there were many date trees in the land).

Further north, we again went to the amphitheater in Caesarea—this time without the pouring rain we had the previous time. We saw much more of it. Traveling further northward we proceeded to Mount Carmel and could see the Jezreel Valley below. Next we toured Meggido. Then on we went to Nazareth where we saw the Absorption Building; this is where Jews migrating from all over the world to Israel come for language training, vocational training if needed, and a place to stay until they can settle in Israel. Jews from all over the world are one of the main imports of Israel.

Tiberias was our next stop for the night; from there we

proceeded to get on a boat and tour part of the Sea of Galilee. At a new museum along the north shore, we got to see the remnants of a boat like Jesus and the disciples used. The restoration process was explained in detail on video and pictures.

From there, we proceeded to the Church of the Sermon on the Mount. To the west of the church was the site where Jesus gave the Sermon on the Mount. Leaving there, we rode through Cana to the Church of the Two Fish and Five Loaves. Outside the church were two Russian professional violinists playing their violins for alms.

Further along the north Galilee shore was St. Peter's Church. While out in the garden we saw a statute of Jesus telling Peter: *Feed my sheep.* We walked down by the seashore and collected a few sea shells and water samples for souvenirs.

Next we visited the city of Jesus—Capernaum. We saw the remnants of Peter's home; an appointment had to be made to visit inside the church that was built over it. Capernaum had some of the most beautiful Bougainvilleas I had ever seen.

Then came my reason for this trip; we went to the Jordan River just below the dam where water empties from the Sea of Galilee into the Jordan River. There is a baptismal site there. This was significant to me as I wanted to be baptized in the Jordan River commemorating what I considered the commissioning of my services to Jesus and the Great Commission. The year before I had made a promise to God that I would do the Great Commission by telling the world about Jesus Christ. The river was hardly flowing because of the dry season, and the water was chilly. Dr. Vaughn did the honor of baptizing me that memorable afternoon. I received a certificate of baptism in the Jordan River. Several of our group were also baptized for various reasons that afternoon.

The following day we went to the ruins of Beit She 'An. There we saw a locust tree like the one from which John the Baptist ate for nourishment. The locust are beans and those beans contain one calorie per bean.

Then we proceeded to Jerusalem and the old walled city and made our way to the Upper Room. Our group sang a couple of praise songs while we were there. Next we went into the shrine of King David's Tomb.

Via bus we made our way to the top of the Mount of Olives and viewed the beautiful city below. Several of us took turns riding the camels for hire. When Buddy Andrews got on the camel, it let out a loud groan. We walked down the Palm Sunday Road to the Jewish cemetery where rocks instead of flowers are placed on top of the graves as a memorial; in the past few flowers were available in Jerusalem. We walked to the Pominus Flevit (Jesus Wept) Church while viewing the Kidron Valley graveyard below. Inside was a spot where it is said that Jesus wept over the city of Jerusalem.

Further down the hill was the Church of All Nations at the Garden of Gethsemane. At the church, we saw priests coming out for Sunday services. We got to pray by the Rock of Agony where Jesus had prayed. Walking outside the church, we went through several old olive trees, many of which were close to 2,000 years old. We went into the garden for a service where Rev. Mike Gilcrease and Dr. Hampton preached.

Leaving the garden, we went via bus to Bethlehem for a little shopping and lunch. We ate shawarma (layers of sliced meats, heated on a rotisserie, sliced, and then placed in a pita bread). We went into the Church of the Nativity. Located there is the spot where Jesus was born.

From there, we proceeded through a courtyard to a room in a building where St. Jerome translated the Bible from Hebrew and Greek to Latin; Scholars say this was done as "job security" for the priests, because the laypeople of that day could not read Latin.

Next we proceeded to a museum showing the model city of old Jerusalem in scale like it was at the time of Jesus. From there we toured the underground tunnel down to the base of the Western Wall, which is on a large table rock forming the foundation of the old temple site.

Nearby was the Western Wall where a Barmitzvah was in progress. Several devout Jews were at the Wailing Wall (Western Wall) reading their scriptures or praying in a to-and-fro motion. For security sake, several armed Israeli soldiers were all over the courtyard there.

Walking up some stairs we came to the Islamic mosque on the Temple Mount, then to the Dome of the Rock which had gold plating on the top portion. Inside is the rock where Abraham is said to have offered Isaac as a sacrifice before God stopped him.

Then we walked over to the Pool of Bethseda where Rev. Craig James preached a sermon and Dr. Al Meredith lead us in singing praise songs.

Following our guides we next walked through the Fortress of Antonio to the Via Dolorosa and on into the Church of the Holy Sepulchre. Inside is where the Greek Orthodox and Catholics believe Jesus was hung on the cross and buried.

Next we proceeded to the church where Peter denied Christ three times and the Pit where Jesus was kept after arrest until the Sanhendrin trial later that morning. The Pit was an answered prophecy in Psalm 88, according to Mike Gilcrease, as he gave a very inspiring mini-sermon about Jesus being there before his later trials on that eventful day.

The next day we went out the Jericho Road (also known as the Wilderness Road) to Masada where we took a cable car to the top. From there we had a great view of the Dead Sea.

Touring Masada we got to see King Herod's palace and swimming pool.

From Masada we traveled to the Dead Sea Resort area where we went swimming. The guides said it was impossible to sink, but I had to prove them wrong. With great effort I dove beneath the surface and paid the price. I got brine and mineral salt into my eyes, nose, and sinuses. I thought I was going to perish. Charles Laughridge and I took a mud bath while there; it is said to be medicinal, but I thought it was awfully messy.

The following morning we went to the Church of John the Baptist near Bethany. From there we then toured the newer part of Jerusalem including the Knisset, the Museum of Israel, then the Museum of the Dead Sea Scrolls.

We went to see the tomb of Lazarus. We got to go down into the tomb where he had been buried. This was a much bigger cavern than I had pictured; it took 75 to 100 steps to get to the bottom. At sites like these the Bible seems to come alive; I could just envision Jesus calling out for Lazarus to come forth. How honored I felt to have the privilege to be able to visit and "live the experiences" of the past.

Our group went back to the old walled city of Jerusalem to the Garden Tomb where we saw the site where Jesus was buried but resurrected after three days. We had a memorial service of the Shared Meal in the garden, Vickie and I were ushers to pass out the bread and wine (grape juice). Mike Gilcrease gave a short sermon on the Last Supper. About that time a cannon went off adjacent to us, just outside the walled city notifying the Muslims that the Ramada fasting was over at 6 p.m.

Half our group thought they had been shot; the sound and vibrations of the cannon shook our teeth.

From Jerusalem we proceeded back to Tel Aviv and flew

back to Athens where most of us began our Mediterranean Cruise to the Greek Isles and Turkey.

First we went to Corinth to see the ruins of the ancient city. We visited the museum there and saw many relics of the Romans and Greeks of centuries past. Down the street was the Corinthian Canal; it is a man-made canal connecting the Gulf of Corinth and the Sardonic Gulf.

We all enjoyed the relaxing cruise as well as the excellent food and the company of Charles and Gayle, Donnie, Mike (Rev. Mike Gilcrease) and several of my church members. We cruised on to the isle of Mykanos and watched the beautiful sunset from the village onshore.

Next we cruised on to the isle of Rhodes and viewed the surroundings from the castle on top. Following that, we cruised on to Ephesus on the mainland of Turkey seeing the old Roman ruins, the coliseum, and the house where John the beloved apostle cared for Mary, the mother of Jesus, until she died.

Next was the historic island of Patmos where John the apostle was kept as a prisoner. While there he wrote the Book of Revelation. We went into the cavern where he is said to have written the book. Then we toured the large church on the mountaintop.

While returning to Athens, we had a big celebration supper on the ship. It was a refreshing and educational trip we all enjoyed.

Chapter 13

The Voodoo Capital of the World Benin, Africa

June 4-19, 2000

One mission adventure doesn't resolve the thirst that creates it. Situated in Gainesville, Florida, Westside Baptist Church has an unquenchable passion for the lost in the world. The church's missions office called and requested that I go to south Benin, Africa, in June 2000. This is the same church-missions group that several from my church had gone with to Thailand in 1999. Although I already had another mission trip scheduled near the same time slot, I talked with Michelle Henley who urgently plead with me to go. I decided to go on what she described as an evangelistic adventure into the jungle where the message of salvation to those who have never heard it awaited.

The pastor from Westside Baptist Church even called me stating that the church was holding a prayer meeting to pray that another doctor would go on their trip. Late that night, after pondering and praying about the trip and after having talked with Michelle, I called her pastor back and told him I would go. I told him that this reminded me of the song: *The Midnight Cry*. So, we had to rush to get my visa to Benin; it arrived two days before I left the U.S.

Jeff and Barbara Singerman had been career Southern Baptist missionaries to Benin, in west Africa, for over fourteen years. They had worked out a partnership with the Westside Baptist Church to travel once or twice a year to work with them. Bill and Margie Belli were also career Southern Baptist missionaries who were working alongside the Singermans. They had been there over six years; they had been brought in to help with the ever-mounting work and possibilities for the additional mission work there.

Finally, I got to meet face-to-face the group from Westside Baptist Church with whom I had been talking. We met in the Miami International Airport on our way to Africa. We boarded an Air France plane and went to Paris, then on to Cotonou, Benin. We arrived in Cotonou on June 5, 2000. After meeting with the Singermans and Bellis, we checked into the Hotel du Lac for the night.

The next morning we had breakfast in the restaurant and watched the locals cast large nets on the lake. We got our meds and supplies approved by the Minister of Health and went on to Allada, about 30 miles north, where the Singermans and Bellis live. We left our luggage at our hotel (Hotel Royame) and went to Bill and Margie Bellis for lunch. Afterwards, we went prayerwalking with Barbara Singerman in D'Agleta village near Allada. We saw firsthand why they call this the Voodoo capital of the world. In the center of the village was a large Voodoo hut where sacrifices are made frequently. Their abodes were baked-clay-and-straw-topped huts which you occasionally see in the National Geographic magazine. The people were friendly and receptive when they found out why we were there. Several of the youth had no clothes on, many of the adults, even the women, had only lower garments on, but some were colorfully dressed.

Then we proceeded to pay a brief visit to the Allada open market. Vegetables, fruits, clothes, and housewares lined the marketplace, but there was a large Voodoo section with animal parts and paraphernalia for Voodoo sacrifices; the area reeked of the stench of dead animal parts. Later I found out how similar this was to the spirituality in parts of this country. They were in dire need of the message of Jesus Christ.

We ate supper at the Hotel Royame and fellowshipped with the Singermans and Bellis before going to the Singermans to get the meds ready for clinic and sandwiches made for lunch.

While relaxing out on the front porch, I asked Barbara to tell me the story behind their being in Africa. Barbara related to me that she was writing a book about that, but would tell me briefly. Jeff and Barbara received their "calling" to be missionaries when Jeff was a youth minister. They got in touch with the International Mission Board and told that entity they were ready to go to Africa—just like that, but they too found out there was a whole lot more to it than that. First, they had to be approved, which they discovered was a real process. Then they went to Paris for a year to learn French. Finally they arrived in Cotonou, Benin to find out that only the business people spoke French, so they had to learn the local dialect, Fon. This, too, took months. Finally, Jeff started the task of youth minister to the territory. When he would hold meetings for the youth, he would schedule Bible study the first half of the day and games, such as volleyball the second half. Much to his surprise the attendees didn't care to play—they wanted to hear more about Jesus.

Jeff was so successful at his youth ministry he soon worked himself out of a job. He had trained young men effectively to carry on the youth work in the country. So Jeff and Barbara turned to the next task at hand which needed doing—

leading the Aziyo people to the Lord. Jeff and Barbara worked so hard that an explosion of new churches occurred. It was so large they couldn't keep up with all the new churches. They didn't have any trained workers to assist with all the new church starts, so Jeff turned to leadership training. He found it imperative that he train men while they were at the same time working in churches.

Before long Jeff and Barbara were so busy they needed assistance. This came in the form of more missionaries such as the Bellis. Jeff found that he did better by teaching pastors for the churches that had been formed and those being formed. Meanwhile Bill Belli would get in his four-wheel-drive vehicle and go to the end of a road or trail and get out and survey the people to see if they would like to have a church started. That is why they called him "the trailblazer".

Then Ryan, Jeff and Barbara's oldest son, started helping by preaching in French and Fon to the people. Barbara told us that having the medical teams come in was very helpful. These drew large crowds where the Gospel could be presented. The group from Westside Baptist had been there the previous year.

I already had begun to admire the Singermans and the Bellis before I even started to work with them. Barbara told me one of the most profound statements I've ever heard, "Jesus keeps me feeling inadequate and uncomfortable at all times, so I will trust in Him always."

The following morning after breakfast we loaded up and went to Azoe-Cada for a full-day clinic. We set up our equipment in a thatched straw hut that was used as a church. The people showed up in large numbers colorfully dressed in their best clothes. Cyprien was my assigned interpreter; he spoke very good English and French, as well as Fon, his native language. He grew up only a few miles from Allada. He had a mannerism that set him aside from all the others. I felt very comfortable with him and admired his love for his own people.

By noon the tropical heat began to take its toll, but we were fortunate to have a portable generator and oscillating fans. We were divided into three groups: Dr. Paul Unkefer, a dermatology resident from Florida, our nurse practitioner, Gayle Barker, and me. We saw many routine things. Some had symptoms of malaria, so we treated them empirically with curative malarial medications, even though we knew that person probably would go right back to his or her environment with the same infectious mosquitoes.

One young male had severe phimosis, so using a penile block, I did a field circumcision right there. The day went fast with the fascinating people coming in as fast as we could see them. Jeff later related to us that this was one of the churches he had helped start.

The following morning we packed up and went to Glossa for a full-day clinic. The word must have gotten out because I couldn't see the end of the line of patients that had come to our clinic. One patient had a split bamboo splint for a broken wrist and it was still markedly swollen, but he refused to let me replace it with a proper plaster-of-Paris splint. Again, we treated many common maladies. We always gave multiple vitamins and usually worm meds to everyone. At the end of the day several of our team used music from a tape recorder to dance with the native people. Their rhythm and grace of movement seemed a little more natural than ours.

The next morning we went to Ayou Ahota for a half-day clinic. Malnutrition was much more apparent at this village. Even a couple of young children were noted to have rickets. On the way back, we saw an occasional common well that people used for a water source. Rain had poured for an hour that morning, helping explain the marked green grass and trees. In the background, we often saw many palm oil trees and coconut palm trees. Bill Belli told us the oil from the palm trees is used to make Palmolive soap. (Palmolive soap is made from palm oil and olive oil according to research on Google.)

After lunch we journeyed to the upper du Lac to visit Ganvie (stilt city). There we found a village of stilt houses out in the middle of the shallow lake where the water in the lake was used for all purposes: drinking, laundering clothes, bathing, and as a bathroom. However, a small island of natural land, with soil added to it by nationals who brought it in by boat, exists there also. On it a deep well has been dug for a safe, drinking-water source. We went by motor boat, but we passed several canoes, some with crude sails. It is believed this city was built on stilts over a century ago to avoid the slave trade.

The following day I learned a lesson not soon to be forgotten. We went to Ahozande and made our clinic in a tin-topped, short, school room with minimal air circulation. The temperature must have been over 105 degrees inside. Drinking several bottles of water seemed to help little. Several of us felt dehydrated by the end of the day. We should have been under the large shade tree outside. One young women presented with multiple necrotic teeth and a draining abscess under the mandible; I proceeded to extract ten teeth—grossing out Gayle, the nurse practitioner. She put up a bright orange plastic tape and told me not to pull teeth across her line.

The next day was Sunday and some of our group went with Jeff to church at Tanta, one of the churches Jeff started. It was baby-dedication day at their church. Jeff seemed relaxed and at ease with the people like he was charter member of the church. In the back were drums and cowbells which were used to make very rhythmic music.

Sunday night we went to the Singermans' house to pack more meds and make sandwiches for clinic the next day. We got into a discussion about witnessing. I told Jeff and Barbara about having just finished the F.A.I.T.H. course. Then it struck me: Why wasn't I doing personal evangelism using the F.A.I.T.H. presentation as a guideline? Right then and there I decided that I would take every opportunity to witness about Jesus and His love for us.

The next day we held a clinic in the school at Tanta because we had determined that the church was too small for our clinic. Jeff had hired the town crier to go around the village and announce the change. We had large numbers of patients that day. I started my personal evangelism and witnessed to eight people who accepted Jesus as Savior that day.

The following day we drove way out into the countryside to Dame village where we worked in mud huts. The mundane medical problems seemed secondary to our real purpose there: winning people to Jesus. I asked myself why I hadn't been doing this previously; I led nine people to accept Jesus that day.

On the way back to our hotel, we passed a Voodoo parade. Two grass huts were moving down the road with someone inside walking them. Jeff told me that this was done to announce that it was Voodoo night. The parade and huts reminded people to stay inside their homes or else—while the Voodoo people did their evil that night. This was really a scare tactic. Their religion was one of fear, not love like Jesus taught.

We held a half-day clinic at Togoudo the next day. I led seven more individuals to accept Jesus as Savior. The names of the seven were given to the missionaries for follow up. That afternoon we had a choice of resting or going out to Lake Toffonou for canoe riding. I chose to go canoeing with Bill

Belli and his two older sons. It was interesting watching the young boys spearing small fish along the shoreline and the men casting nets out in the lake. I bought one of the casting nets, but found it very difficult to throw it as graceful every time as the men in the lake did.

The last day of clinic we went to Devou Kanmey for a full day of clinic. We saw a lot of patients. More importantly I led eight more to accept Jesus as Savior. Cyprien was an excellent interpreter and very attentive with the Gospel presentation for salvation. I told him that he and his friends should be presenting the Gospel to all their friends like we had been doing the last few days.

The following day, after all the clinics had been finished, we drove to Ouidah to see the Musee D'Histore De Ouidah (an old Portugese fort made into a museum) to hear and see the real history of slavery. More slaves left from Ouidah than anywhere in west Africa. They left from what was called the Port of No Return on ships to various places in the world. Departure occurred after the captured people were "acclimated" in a building approximately 75 by 200 feet. The guide said approximately one-third of the slaves died there, one-third died on the crowded ships taking them away, and only one-third finally made it to their destinations. The people were captured by other Africans and sold into slavery for very little. The guide said no foreigners captured the people and then sold them as slaves. Following through the museum and hearing the real story was such a tragedy of history. We went down by the seashore to see a large monument called LaPorte Du Nonretour (the Port of No Return) commemorating these events.

On the way back, Barbara told me more about her book and asked me to help think of a good title.

About midnight, we flew out of Cotonou to Paris where we spent the next thirty hours. We toured the city in a bus, seeing the Seine River, Notre Dame Cathedral, Senate House, Arc de Triomphe, Effiel tower, and several other historic spots.

Several of us arose early the next morning and went via subway to the Louvre Museum (equivalent to the Smithsonian Institute in the U.S.). We saw the original Mona Lisa and the Venus de Milo statue, and many other interesting artifacts, portraits, etc.

I thoroughly enjoyed this trip and decided to go again the next year—mainly because I felt I needed to do more personal evangelism, which I missed out on the first part of this trip. The Singermans and Bellis were such gracious hosts.

CHAPTER 14

South Mexico

June/July 2000

While I was taking the F.A.I.T.H. course at Broadmoor Baptist Church in Shreveport, my sister, Linda, a member there, signed me up for the annual mission trip to the Mexican Indian Training Center (MITC) in Cordoba in southern Mexico. After receiving approval from Dr. Larry Williams who was coordinating the trip from the church, I recruited Rosemary and Buddy Andrews and Sherman French (Ph.D. in Education).

Rosemary and Buddy stopped by my house the afternoon I returned home from Benin and picked up a large box of meds and supplies I had left over from that mission trip. They were having a medicine-packing party, but I was just too exhausted to go.

Broadmoor Baptist Church had gone all out to prepare us for the Mexico trip. The church provided Spanish-language-training sessions so I went. But I have to admit it: I'm foreign language impaired.

Our group drove via bus from the church to the International Airport at Houston where we then flew to Vera Cruz. From there we took a bus to Fortin and stayed at the Fortin de las Flores Hotel.

The following morning we all met in the courtyard for a

brief worship service and introductory messages by Dan Hall, head of MITC, Dr. Larry Williams, mission group coordinator, and Dr. Chuck Pourciau, pastor of Broadmoor Baptist Church. We then separated into the groups for which we had volunteered. Rosemary, Buddy, Sherman and I had volunteered to go out to the "country", a six-hour drive southwest of Cordoba almost to Guatemala, for the week. Dr. Stephen Patton, nephrologist from Shreveport, was our group leader.

As we traveled south for the next six hours, we saw a lot of the countryside; at one point a bridge was out due to the heavy rain the previous night. This only caused a minor delay in our journey to Megone. I was told there were no phones there and only sparse electrical supply as we were so far out in the country. We took up residence in an empty house close to our sponsoring pastor. The women were assigned to one room and the men to the other two rooms. We slept on air mattresses. I took over the job of assigning the order when each person would take a "shower" by soaping down and then pouring a cold bucket of water over his or her head and body—a bit refreshing.

It was very quiet out in the country except for the occasional sound of a cricket or a sporadic snore that night. The next morning and every morning thereafter we went next door to the home of Felix, our sponsoring pastor, and had breakfast consisting of fresh tortillas, fruit, eggs, toast, and cereal. It was very filling.

The first day of work we went to Bocadel Monde for the first half of the day and Basoreal for the remainder of the day. We saw a lot of patients. Having learned my lesson in Benin, I asked everyone I saw if he or she was a Christian, then if Jesus lived in his or her heart. If not, I proceeded to give the person a modified F.A.I.T.H. presentation. Several accepted Jesus as Savior.

I was not the only one individually evangelizing for Jesus. The pastors were presenting the Gospel for salvation purposes, also. Ron, a local pastor, was my interpreter; he was so easy to work with and enjoyed my evangelistic efforts.

We worked in a church building in Boca del Monde; in Basoreal we worked under tents and under the edge of the buildings where we were located. We saw patients until 8 p.m., then were treated to a delicious home-cooked meal.

The following day was Sunday so we went via bus to the church at San Juan Guichiacobi. Immediately after church we went down the street for lunch at the home of one of the pastors. After lunch we briefly explored the village center and the Catholic Church which looked a century old. Then we went back to the same church and held clinic until 8 p.m. so we could see everyone who wanted to be seen. Sherman worked at the triage station and began to pick up some forgotten Spanish and a whole lot more. Rosemary worked in the pharmacy. Buddy was an assistant to Dr. Steve Hooper, our dentist from Bossier City.

Every morning before breakfast at our house Dr. Patton led us in a devotional. Monday morning we went to Ecino for an all-day clinic. Buddy Andrews daily had been witnessing to our bus driver, Phillipe Barjonah Sanchez, and that morning he accepted Jesus as Savior. I couldn't tell who was happier, the bus driver or Buddy. The weather remained hot every day as usual; the only cool part of the day was between 5 and 8 a.m. We worked outside under a large mango tree, moving as the sun changed positions in the sky. We ate lunch and supper with the people there that day. It was excellent.

On the morning of July 4th we had a special devotion praising God for our freedom and his graceful mercy on us. We went to Piedra Blanca for a full-day clinic. Again we worked outside under the mango trees near the local church. I went inside the church to do a few minor surgical procedures. The people were very receptive and many accepted Jesus as Savior because of our personal evangelism. The names were recorded for the local pastors. One pastor said his church had more than doubled in size since the medical team visited the previous year. Sherman told me I was giving Pastor Ron, my interpreter, witnessing lessons because of all the people who had accepted Jesus as Savior.

The last clinic day we went to the nearby Mogone Baptist Church. Again we saw many people. One thing that really stood out that day was when I presented the Gospel to one older man who vehemently resisted. He said there was no God or Jesus, and when he died he would be gone. Roughly translated, he said he "didn't believe in that stuff." That was the first time I have experienced such rejection. Fortunately, many did accept Jesus as Savior. At the end of the clinic we celebrated with a big cake Dr. Patton's birthday. He was quite surprised. Then we drove back to Cordoba to join the others.

The following morning we went shopping in downtown Cordoba where we bought a few souvenirs. Some of us went into the large Catholic Church in the town center. It was beautiful.

The whole group then met at the MITC where we took a tour of the facility. Rev. Dan Hall was the director of the MITC, founded by his father, Dr. Dan Hall of Shreveport.

The compound consisted of dormitories for men and women, a worship center, a gymnasium, and training facilities. Here the Mexican Indians were trained in at least two vocations, a musical instrument, and evangelism before returning to their own village. This facility is supported significantly by people in Shreveport.

A very lengthy praise service was held in the worship center. Even Dr. Pourciau said, "My dad taught me long years ago to never let a service last longer than the bottom could last to sit."

We then went to Vera Cruz for a night out on the beach, Unfortunately, we never got to enjoy it in the day time because of lack of time. We had to leave for the airport before dawn the next morning to fly back to Houston, then via bus back to Shreveport.

From my perspective the mission trip was excellent. I applaud the MITC for its dedicated work and service to the local people. Also I was very pleased with the people from Broadmoor Baptist Church for their hospitality to us and the service they rendered to the MITC and the people of Mexico.

CHAPTER 15

Brazil
Teresina and Caxius de Sol

August 2000

In the spring of 2000, I was asked by Dr. Johnny Baker, assistant pastor of Calvary Baptist Church, to accompany him and a group on a mission trip to Brazil. The group would be going to Teresina (northern Brazil) for three days to work with IMB missionaries Vic and Sharon Johnston, then fly south to Caxius de Sol to work with IMB missionaries John and Kathy Vaughn. Johnny knew that I was making a lot of mission trips and invited me. I agreed if Vickie, my wife, could go. He agreed.

Dr. Johnny Baker and his wife had served as IMB missionaries to Brazil for almost ten years and spoke Portugese like Brazilians. The Baker's son was getting married to the Vaughn's daughter in the near future. We were going to do evangelism work and pay them a visit also.

We started holding meetings about every two weeks for two months before the trip. We were oriented to what to expect and able to meet everyone who had been chosen to go on the team. This was strictly an evangelism trip, not a medical-missions trip like I usually do. The other pastor who had been invited had to drop out for family reasons, so I suggested that

Rev. Sonny DePrang and his wife, Jackie, be asked to go. They were contacted, prayed about it, and not long afterwards agreed to go. Vickie initially did not want to go, but the DePrangs helped convince her it was the thing to do.

We continued our preparations and meetings for going until we finally were ready to depart on August 7, 2000. We flew to Miami and then to Brazil. We stayed at the Palacio Do Rio Hotel in Teresina where we met with the Johnstons. The following day we drove several miles out into the countryside where the Johnstons had been ministering to the people. We went to a local school where Dottie Mobley dressed up like a clown and entertained the children. Vickie got to play her flute also. The children were very enthusiastic about our visit and many previously had never seen North Americans.

Later Sonny and I gave spiritual messages or sermons to some of the adults at the school. That night I gave a sermon on salvation and five accepted Jesus as Savior. The following day we visited another school to give the good news of Jesus. The children were excited to have Americans (from the U.S.) visit them; they were very receptive to the Gospel.

In Teresina, it was winter, but warm daily to the lower 90's; it was only 200 miles from the equator. Leaving our gracious hosts, Vic and Sharon, we flew to Porto Alegre, which was way down in south Brazil, then on to Caxius de Sol, which is not far from Paraguay. There it was 60 degrees colder in comparison to Teresina. We met with the Vaughns before going to our hotel. The water in the shower initially was freezing cold. Because we had very little heat in the room and were not accustomed to the big change in temperature, that night we slept in our clothes and piled on all the covers we had.

We were introduced to a married couple who were physicians in Caxius de Sol. They took Vickie and me to the public hospital, then to the private hospital where they did most of their work. They were very pleasant and even showed us around the nearby public park.

The next day we visited one of the local schools where we mingled with the school children. Our group did Vacation Bible School activities for the children. I made a few balloons out of some surgical gloves and drew faces on them; the children absolutely loved these.

The following day was Sunday. We went to church at the Primeiral Greja Batista Church. Sonny and I gave our testimonies during the Sunday-School hour. Johnny gave the sermon in Portugese during the worship hour. Afterwards, we all went out to a restaurant for lunch. That night we went to a different church where I gave a brief testimony, Vickie and Jackie sang, Vickie played her flute, and Sonny gave the evangelical message. The Brazilian children sang for us. It was a delightful service and well received by the people.

The following day we went to the edge of the city and prayerwalked the village. Later we visited door to door inviting all the people to the local "cell" church which was in one of the local's garage. Surprisingly, the turnout that night was great—standing room only. A number of cell churches later united together to form a formal church. Starting with small cell groups, then merging groups together is the best way to plant new churches in the communities there, according to the Vaughns.

On the way back to Porto Alegre, we stopped by a German town and did some shopping in a mall. We had lunch at a local "home restaurant" which was just excellent. We then flew to Sao Paulo on the way back to the U.S.

It was a very good trip—a little out of my line of expertise, but interesting and rewarding as well. The Bakers made it a very enjoyable trip and the fellowship was great with all the team members.

Chapter 16

Return to Benin, Africa
June 2001

After preparing long distance with the group from Westside Baptist Church in Gainesville, Florida, and determined to return to Benin to do more evangelism with the Singermans and Bellis, I finally flew to Philadelphia on the way to Benin and met the group there in the airport. Michelle Henley and Clyde Pfiffer were again leading the team. We flew overnight to Paris and then to Cotonou, Benin. We were met at the airport by the Singermans and Bellis and welcomed once again. This time my luggage arrived with our plane; the previous year it arrived a day late.

We spent the first night in the Baptist Guest House in Cotonou, went shopping the next day in the city, then drove to Allada 30 miles north to our hotel, the Royame Allada, where we had stayed the previous year. For hours we sorted and packed meds in preparation for clinic the next day. We were back in Ayizo country, the people group to whom the Singermans and Bellis ministered. Jeff and Barbara had been working for years with this people group. Many new churches had been formed. Jeff stayed busy training the pastors of these churches in how to minister to their people. The Bellis had joined the Singermans because of the tremendous amount of work that needed to be done.

On June 20, 2001, we went to Azoe-Hounwahounou and

saw about 100 patients. This year I was ready for the dental caries and abscessed teeth. I brought my newly acquired dental instruments I got from my dentist who lives next door. He gave advice on how to do the dental blocks.

Voodoo abounded in the village, according to Jeff and Barbara. Nevertheless, I led three to accept Jesus as Lord and Savior. Kevin Singerman, second son of Barbara and Jeff, was my assistant and interpreter. He loved helping and seemed interested in becoming a doctor one day.

Dr. Jay Fricker of the pediatric department at the University of Florida was my roommate and working partner. This was the first time he had been to Africa. He was very enthusiastic about the "clinics" where we were working.

The next day we got out our backpacks and brought the powdered meals Bill Belli had asked us to bring. We readied for a hike to Ci country. No roads to the village past a certain point existed. We went by four-wheel-drive vehicles as far as we could go, then we set out on foot for Ci country. We walked about three kilometers through jungle and occasionally open fields, noticing where an occasional vehicle had attempted to go further before stopping so the people onboard could set out on foot like we were doing. We finally came to a small river (Koufou) which was now swollen from the recent rains. Scott, our point man, decided to put his gear in a large dish pan and wade across the river. Suddenly he disappeared from site with only the pan floating where he had been. After he reappeared, we knew that option was out. The other choices were to ride in the small canoe and get our bottoms wet or put our gear, including cameras, into the canoe and hold on to the side of the canoe until we got to the other bank. I chose the second option to keep my backpack and camera dry.

After we finally all crossed the river, we changed into dry

clothes and marched another three kilometers to the Ci village through hundreds of acres of cultivated corn fields. The weather was hot and humid with the sun bearing down, making the occasional breeze seem heavenly.

The village itself was a trip back in time to the 1700s. The huts were made with grass and oil-palm stems. They had no electricity and no common source of clean water. This was deep into Voodoo country. The people stared at us like they had never seen white people and initially seemed very suspicious of us.

Amazingly, the people, however, were dressed like their neighbors in the city many miles away. We were introduced to the village chief and his people by Gabriel, Jeff Singermans' night guard, who spoke their dialect. Then we proceeded to set up clinic in the grass huts and worked for four hours before we stopped to put up our small tents for the night. Bill Belli's oldest son, who came with us, decided to be my tentmate. We set our tent outside in the yard, while the others set up theirs under a large grass hut.

We boiled our drinking water and poured it on our prepared powdered meals for supper. The village cooked us a giant container of rice. Because some of our members contracted amoebic dysentery the previous year, I was careful to avoid any village food or water.

I found out that our tent was situated in a barnyard site. We had pigs, goats, dogs, and later chickens come by our tent all night to entertain us. It was a good thing we had a tent because rain fell early that morning before sunrise. We also had more than enough mosquitoes for the entire village.

We held clinic again the next day. Kevin was my assistant and one of my interpreters; Judy, Gabriel's daughter, was the other. We had to go from English to French through Kevin and

French to a Fon dialect through Judy and then back again to communicate. This didn't seem to matter as many people were receptive to treatment and very receptive to the Gospel. I led at least thirteen people to accept the Lord.

We saw various diseases. One of the main problems was infected calluses on the hands and especially on the feet. The people would work in the wet corn fields all day and macerate their skin; at night it would dry out and crack to the basal layer of skin or below into the subcutaneous tissue, frequently getting infected. This reminded me of my Vietnam days seeing "jungle rot" on the Marines whose feet frequently were wet for days. I showed the people how to cut off the thick callus to the lower level of skin and asked them to keep it trimmed to avoid the crevice formation.

There were other conditions such as chronic spleenomegaly from chronic malaria. We also saw a lot of the usual things such as pain from working all day every day. One lady had witch-doctor scars (keloids) on her from face to feet, particularly on the back and abdomen where she had received "treatment". Thank God she accepted Jesus as Savior!

The weather was stifling with humidity and heat, but we worked so diligently with the people I tried to ignore that. The appreciation from the people and the many who accepted Jesus as Savior seemed to make it a bearable situation.

That afternoon one of the native people dressed in voodoo garb put on a show for us. We held a village meeting prior to leaving, and the people expressed happiness we had come their way. Where there had been only two Christians in the village before we arrived Jeff and Barbara sent me an email three weeks later stating that a church had been started the next week and 60 people were present. Later I received an email in which Jeff and Barbara said they baptized 27 people when they spent the weekend in Ci country. I know that the International Mission Board loves this kind of report; that's what it is all about!

We got to rest and tour the next two days; it was exhausting going out to Ci country, but very rewarding. As we had the previous year, we went to the Ouida Museum and the Port of No Return. Sunday we went to the Allada Baptist Church where several people were baptized, including Cyprien, my interpreter from the previous year. He had seen me witness to dozens of people. He never said anything nor did I think to ask if he was a Christian. What a delight to have him now as a Christian brother in Christ.

The next four days we held clinic daily going to (1) Alga on June 25, (2) Tuffo Tukon on June 26, (3) Akajamey on June 27, and (4) Tori Avarney on June 28. Each day was hot and humid. Some days were worse than others. Dr. Fricker developed nausea, vomiting, and diarrhea and by June 28 had to stay in the hotel; he said each day just beat him. I really learned to like him as a friend, roommate, and colleague.

Each day I got to fulfill my commission—telling all that would listen about Jesus. Every day during clinic several accepted Christ.

It was an exceptionally hot and sweltering day when we were in Tuffo Tukon. We were working in grass huts with minimal circulation of air. One patient had a guinea worm under the skin. Not being very familiar with this tropical parasite I asked Bill Belli how to treat this. He said the natives soak in water until the worm sticks its head or body out and then they grab it and wind it around a stick slowly for the next two or three days so as not to break the 24 to 36 inch worm. I didn't have that luxury of time; I cut down to the encased worm and twisted it out with a hemostat; then resutured the wound. Not

long after this, I excised a second guinea worm.
One day we were in a school building with a tin roof only 8-to-9 feet high. We were so hot. I found out it is so much better to work out under a big shade tree.
The next evening we were going to see Gonvie, the city built on stilts out in du Loc, but Jeff wanted us two doctors to go see a lady missionary in the hospital in Cotonou and give a second opinion about her abdominal pain, so we agreed. After talking and examining her, it was not real clear what was going on. Suzanne Crocker, the missionary, wanted to be medivaced to Abidjon, Ivory Coast—a two-hour flight away where there is a large Canadian hospital—because she was uncertain about treatment of a surgical disease in Benin. The Benin surgeon came in and refused to sign the order to medivac her out of the country. He stated that his clinic had just as good or better treatment than anywhere in Africa. Suzanne become almost angry with the doctor and asked if I could do her surgery if she required it. I reminded her that surgery is a highly territorial thing and that we were playing on the Benin surgeon's turf.
An ultrasound was ordered which basically ruled out the worry of an ureteral calculus or twisted ovarian cyst. Suzanne began to hurt worse and worse in the right lower quadrant and it became apparent an appendectomy was essential. I asked the African surgeon if I could be his first assistant and he agreed. This was the best I could have hoped for under the circumstances. Anyway I agreed to miss my trip to Paris and stay the next three days until the next flight so I could help with Suzanne's surgery. The family and other missionaries were most pleased that I stayed.
The African surgeon and I took Suzanne to the operating room (a circa 1950 setting for an operating room, but the best

in Benin). We did a routine appendectomy through a tiny right lower quadrant incision. She did well, but had to stay in the hospital three days to be treated also for malaria.

I became dehydrated the next day and thought I was coming down with malaria. But after 5 liters of water I felt much better by the end of the day.

Working with this year's team was just great; I hated to part from the group, but know they understood about other obligations. The Crockers and other missionaries were so appreciative.

I left Monday night and traveled over 8,000 miles in the next 29 hours to get home to my one and only; she was happy to see me too. I think she developed occult compression fractures of her cervical, thoracic, and lumbar vertebrae from my hugging her so hard and long on arrival back home. I had never been away from her that long: 15 days, 8 hours, 35 minutes, and 10.339 seconds.

What a great trip! The Singermans and Bellis are the greatest when it comes to serving on medical missions in places like Africa. They have become life-long friends. I still correspond with them. Barbara said never come to Africa unless you are ready for an adventure and to have your patience severely tested.

Barbara was finishing up her book, but didn't have a title about their missionary story and struggles. Her book finally came out two years later with the title *Beyond Surrender* chosen by her publisher, Hannibal Books. I highly recommend it to anyone who thinks about going on the mission field or even doing short-term missions. It is a jewel of a book. (To order visit www.hannibalbooks.com or call Hannibal Books at 1-800-747-0738.)

CHAPTER 17

Rio de Janeiro
The Beautiful City

November 2001

In October 2001 I called Blessings International in Tulsa, Oklahoma, to order medicine for another mission trip. As I talked with the receptionist there, she asked who referred me to them. When she found out it was Dr. Dewey Dunn, she related what a great trip and results he had just accomplished in Rio de Janeiro, Brazil. He had just called her wanting more supplies for another trip there. I was so amazed at the number of patients and converts she cited that I decided to call Dr. Dunn that night at home.

I had met Dewey and Bobbie at a recent Baptist Medical Dental Fellowship Meeting. I called him and inquired about the trip and asked if he could use another doctor to go to Rio de Janeiro. He said he would love to have me if I could get a visa before a group from the Tennessee Baptist Convention left in two weeks.

The next day I called the Brazil embassy in Washington, D.C. I was told the embassy could process my visa in 10 days or less, so I filled out and faxed the forms, then sent my passport, pictures, and fees. Two days before we left I received my visa. The travel agency that the Tennessee Baptist Convention used was very gracious in getting me airplane tickets also.

Dr. Dewey Dunn has coordinated many trips. Three years previous he was honored by the International Mission Board for having done over 50 medical-mission trips. He tries to do four to five mission trips a year. He certainly has been a role model for me to follow.

A rather large group—39—finally assembled and flew to Rio de Janeiro. We were taken to the Luxor Continental Hotel. It was a very pretty and nice hotel one block from Copacobana Beach. There we met the sponsoring IMB missionaries, Sharon and Ray Fairchild. They had been working in Rio de Janeiro for several years and had concluded that bringing in medical teams was a great approach for evangelism in the local areas. They said this was a significant way to attract people to the local churches where the clinics were held. The missionaries gave us an idea of what was to happen during the next week.

Every morning at 5:30 a.m. I would get up and prior to breakfast go to a Bible study and prayer meeting with Dr. Dunn. Then we would have breakfast, which was always so delicious with the fresh fruits of Brazil—melon, papaya, pineapple, kiwi, cantaloupe, and several other native fruits.

At the introductory meeting, we met all the group members. Our interpreters were introduced to us as well. There were eleven doctors and only one dentist, Dr. Charles Van Diver from DeWitt, Texas, who was 80-years old. Dr. Dunn asked for a volunteer to help Dr. Van Diver extract teeth. Having done this on previous mission trips in Africa, I volunteered.

Our group went out into the suburbs or *vallelas* in Bon Sucesso to the Second Baptist Church which is out in the "slum areas" of the city. The first three hours in the dental clinic I attentively listened and looked on to see the finer techniques of dental extractions as taught by Dr. Van Diver. We didn't have time to do corrective dental care. He told me he was going to "learn me something"—if I was to be "taught something" I might forget.

Soon I was on my own but had his advice and assistance nearby. I did not have an interpreter so I either asked Roger (a native Brazilian interpreter not assigned to me) or memorized a few terms like *abre bocca* (open your mouth), *fascia bocca* (close your mouth), and *proximo* (next). The natural phenomenon or reaction of pain was universal in language, so I didn't have to ask. I already knew how to do the local blocks like a palatine block, but had not mastered the aveolar block until properly taught by Dr. Van Diver. I also learned all the proper instruments to use in the complete dental set that Dr. Van Diver had brought with him. Sara, Dr. Van Diver's assistant of 32 years, assisted him; Roger was his interpreter. I had neither assistant nor interpreter; I used a head light, which was quite ample.

By the end of the day, I was extracting teeth at a satisfactory rate; occasionally I would break off a posterior molar. Dr Van Diver said it was just part of the procedure and he would drill or excise the fragments out for me. It was truly an educational session.

One day in the pastor's office I did two circumcisions on young patients who had severe phimosis (stricture of the foreskin). This earned me the title of "Rabbi Bailey".

We remained very busy and rarely took a break, but when we did I would go visit the other stations. At the eye clinic many people were made happy by getting glasses for the very first time. Occasionally, you could see a big tear rolling down a smiling face. Justina Rivera, R.N., was working there diligently. We would meet on future trips because she works with Dr. Dewey Dunn in Nashville. Elaine Jackson and Sharon Dobbs were also helping at the eye clinic. At the end of the eye-clinic line was a retired missionary to Brazil for over 50 years, Clara Williams. She was still active in part-time missionary work. She presented the Gospel to the patients and many accepted Jesus as Savior.

Dr. Everett Lee, endocrinologist from Oklahoma and my roommate, was busy in the medical clinic along with Susan, an internal medicine doctor who worked in an emergency room in Alabama, and Dr. Dunn. They were doing individual evangelism, but occasionally Susan would fill the whole room with patients and give a Gospel presentation and many would accept Jesus as Savior.

Dr. Gary Bohn was also in the medical section seeing patients and presenting the Gospel. Nearby was Dr. Pierre Berry, native Brazilian who left for the U.S. 25 years ago. He eventually trained to be a family practitioner. He was back for the first time. He initially had trouble with his Portugese, but it returned rapidly.

In the pediatric section were Dr. Bill Skinner, a recently retired IMB missionary to Paraguay; Dr. Gary Alexander, family practitioner from Georgia; and Susan McGann, mid-wife from Fort Bragg in North Carolina. (Susan was an assistant in the pediatric clinic.) Dr. Skinner later invited all of us to visit Paraguay in 2002 to celebrate the 50th anniversary of the Baptist Hospital in Asuncion, Paraguay in 2002.

In the pharmacy were five registered pharmacists. With all the doctors writing prescriptions, all five were kept busy.

Being a general surgeon, I was requested to remove a cyst from the chest wall of a patient, but when I went to get the patient, Brenda, IMB missionary to Brazil, said, "Wait, I have something more important first; she needs to accept Christ as Savior, then you can cut off the cyst." This was the most profound and meaningful statement made all week while I was there.

During the week, I had perfected all the blocks and had been "learned" what proper instruments to use to extract each tooth. With proper elevation and proper application of the instrument to the neck of the tooth instead of the crown, I got to where I rarely broke off a tooth anymore . By the end of the week I was quite proficient at extracting teeth. By being so busy extracting teeth and not having an interpreter I didn't get to present the Gospel to the patients until the very last patient. I borrowed Roger and presented the Gospel to that patient and she accepted Jesus as Savior.

In our morning sessions Rev. Gary Haskins, the only minister on the trip, gave devotionals during group time.

That week we saw over 2,800 people in the clinics; 714 of them accepted Jesus as Savior. This had to be the most evangelistic team I had ever worked with to date.

The last day we went out on a boat to cruise the bay. One of our pharmacists, Mr. McGough, was talking with our guide and during the tour lead her to the Lord.

A similar incidence took place the previous day. I had sent Shirley Hester, our dental hygienist, back to the hotel because she became too hot and her blood pressure was rising. When she got back to the hotel she called the front desk and told them she wanted the highest ranking person to come to her room to talk with her. She ended up leading that lady to the Lord.

After the bay tour, we went to lunch at a restaurant which specialized in cooked meats: roast beef, chicken, ribs, Brahman bull hump, pork, etc. Then we took the trolley to

Corcovado (humpback) Mountain to see the Christ the Redeemer statue. Everyone in Rio de Janeiro knew about Christ because of that statue, which made it easier to lead them to the Lord. Christ the Redeemer statue was celebrating its 70th year.

From the top of the Corcovado is one of the most beautiful sites to look out over the bay and see Sugar Loaf Mountain, Copacobana Beach, the surrounding mountains, and the city. The view is astounding. No wonder this is one of the most visited places in the world—it is called "the beautiful city".

I thoroughly enjoyed this educational-and-spiritual mission trip; I felt I matured as a *dentista* (Portugese for dentist); I loved working with the people on the medical team. I have always said when you go on a mission trip with Dr. Dewey Dunn it will be good. I met people there with whom I am still going on medical-mission trips.

CHAPTER 18

The Trip to Maracaibo Venezuela

January 2002

In late summer 2002, Dr. Charles Walker once again called on me to help with a medical-mission trip involving some LSU Med students. This time we would go to Maracaibo, Venezuela.

Dr. Walker had been conferring with Harvey and Sharon McCone, who were serving as IMB missionaries to Venezuela with a group called FUNDABREZ (the Foundation Medical/Social for Baptist in Zulia) in Maracaibo. This project had been going for five years in Maracaibo. A partnership program had been accomplished with eight churches in Alabama. This program had treated over 23,000 patients with 4,400 decisions for Christ.

Charles and I met with the McCones in south Arkansas prior to going to Maracaibo to get details of the proposed trip, I had really enjoyed our trip to Mexico in 1999 with some students from LSU Med School.

Ester Hall helped Charles coordinate our trip from Shreveport. I ordered some meds for our trip from CrossLinks International and M.A.P. International. Prior to going, Charles had me meet with the students.

Via email I corresponded with the McCones to find out further information. I was asked by Sharon to email Dr. Frank Page who gave me an idea of what to expect and advised I correspond with a pharmacist, Riley Brice, who was considered to be one of the most knowledgeable people in the world on mission projects. So I emailed Riley and he gave me further advice on how to estimate the amount of meds we would use for the number of doctors seeing patients in so many days. He also sent me a CD for labeling meds in Spanish.

Finally our group, including my wife, Vickie, and I flew through Miami International Airport where I saw "Neon Deion" (Deion Sanders). I persuaded him to pose for a picture with me. We then flew to Maracaibo and went to our hotel, Hotel del Lago, which was very nice. The following day we met at the McCone's home to separate and count meds for the clinics. Rachel Richardson, one of the students, was upstairs complaining of right lower abdominal pain. I was asked to evaluate her. She seemed to have point right lower quadrant abdominal tenderness, so I determined that she needed to go to the hospital emergency room for evaluation. That left the other students—Stacey Conville, Brian Smith, and Jo Nida along with Don Salyer, our pharmacist, nurse practitioner Romona Green, and Vickie—working with the meds.

We went to the emergency room where it literally took hours and hours to get things done. Eventually it was determined after X-rays, lab work, an ultrasound of the abdomen, and finally a CT of the abdomen that she needed to be admitted for observation. Approximately 9 hours later we finally got back to our hotel.

The following morning was Sunday, so we went to the Mission Puerto Alto Gracia for church services, which were very enjoyable.

Monday and Tuesday we visited the FUNDABREZ Clinics, but did no work until the McCones got back in country, then we started clinic work at Puerto Alto Gracia Mision Church.

Between Dr. Morse, the Venezuelan doctors, Romona Green, the med students and me we saw a steady stream of patients. The pharmacy was soon very busy with all the prescriptions, especially since they had to be labeled in Spanish and counted and placed in small bags.

On the way back to our hotel that evening, we stopped for supper at the *Pollo Krispie* (Krispy Chicken), a fast food restaurant. While waiting for our food we were approached by a boy, approximately nine years of age, wanting to sell us some chocolate candy. He was dressed poorly. No one seemed interested in buying any candy from him until Hector, one of our interpreters, found out that he lived across the street and couldn't go home until he had sold all his candy. So we then bought all his candy. We even bought him some supper to eat with us.

We had clinic at Mision Puerto Alto Gracia Church again the next day. This time a long line of patients was awaiting us. The medical students did well with supervision and loved the hands-on clinical experience. We saw many patients for routine things that day and swamped the pharmacy again with all the prescriptions we wrote.

On January 11th, thirteen nurses from the Baptist Nursing Fellowship joined our group at the hotel. Also the group from Cuba that Dr. Walker had arranged to travel to Venezuela from the Cuba Baptist Missions—Dr. Patricio Penalver, Dr. Milton Conde, dentist, Dr. Elena Calcines, and nurse Hida Pina—joined us.

Saturday the entire group went just past the city limits to a

Yukpa village. The people there were very poor and depended for the most part on salvaging things from the city dump for survival. We had fellowship with them at town center. The nurses from the Baptist Nursing Fellowship gave them many gifts, mostly hygiene items such as soap, shampoo, toothbrushes, and toothpaste.

The following day was Sunday, so we went to the Iglesia Bautisa Fuente de Amor (Fountain of Love). We ate lunch in the church courtyard afterwards and were entertained by a 12-year-old lad who sang beautifully (a young Enrico Iglesias).

That afternoon we went to *Sina Mica Rio* for a boat tour of the river. We went up river to where we were surprised to see a large banner out in front of one of the waterfront homes welcoming the Louisiana BMDF. We fellowshipped with the people there, then toured a mission church on the river bank. Along the river were large mangrove trees with roots dropping from their limbs into the river. The background jungle was so thick no one could travel through it. It was a refreshing tour.

On Monday, we returned to Fuente de Amor church for clinic. The Baptist Nursing Fellowship group administered immunizations. Drs. Fred Loper and Tom Ginn had joined our group by then. They would stay the rest of the time that the students were there. We really saw large numbers of patients and sent a large volume of prescriptions to the pharmacy to fill.

That night we all went to the McCone's home for supper and fellowship. A good time was had by all that attended; the food was very good.

The next two days we worked at the Neuva Esperanza (New Hope) church; it was an open-air building so we were able to see everyone in action. Joyce Keith was working in triage; Cullen Keith and Charles were working in the eye clinic, the students were alongside the doctors working as independently as possible, and the pharmacy staff were trying to keep up with us.

The students were a joy to work with. They seemed to get a lot out of the trip. They had gotten to do work like the doctors they were training to be.

This was a unique mission trip in several ways. The McCones and Dr. Charles Walker had set up the trip months earlier. Then Dr. Walker invited members of the Cuban Medical Dental Fellowship to come along. (Dr. Walker has worked to help set up the Cuban Medical Dental Fellowship over the past three years.) This was the first time since Fidel Castro came to power in 1962 that missionaries of any type have been allowed to leave Cuba. So, two missionary groups from two different countries came to minister to a third—a little different one would have to say.

We held eleven days of clinics seeing close to 5,000 patients between the doctors, dentists, and eye clinics. Close to 450 made professions of faith in Christ during these days. The different churches are to follow up with each individual about his/her decision.

Most of the days were very warm. We always seemed to have more patients to see than we actually could. But, the people were so grateful. They otherwise couldn't have afforded the clinic visits, medications, teeth extractions, eye exams and eyeglasses, or minor surgeries performed. The medications we obtained from CrossLink International and M.A.P. International ran short by the middle of the second week. It just so happened that a member of the FUNDABREZ happened to work for a pharmaceutical company and that organization stepped in with help when we needed $1,000 more of medications. The Baptist Nursing Fellowship, which had arrived the second week and worked with us, just happened to have $1,000 for needed supplies. The Lord does provide, doesn't He? I helped procure the meds and supplies, but had no idea we would be seeing this many people—twice what the McCones had estimated.

The idea of the mission trip was great; so was the end result. Most everyone seemed fully satisfied about the trip.

CHAPTER 19

Land of the Guarani Paraguay

2002, 2004

As was promised by Dr. Bill Skinner, the Paraguay Baptist Medical Center Foundation's invitation to Asuncion, Paraguay, for the 50th anniversary of the Baptist Hospital there came in time for adequate preparation. Dr. John Bryant and Al and Peggy Hethcock were instrumental in securing the invitations. This was to be the first volunteer medical team to visit Paraguay. A group of forty was planned, but sixty-three went due to the enthusiastic promotion.

Our group flew to Asuncion and immediately went to our hotel (Portal de Sol) where we were introduced to the missionaries serving in Paraguay. That evening we went to the Baptist Hospital for a reception and celebration. There we learned the history of the Baptist Hospital and Dr. William Skinner's dedicated work to get the hospital started 50 years earlier. He was an IMB missionary to Paraguay for 38 years. It was very interesting to learn about Dr. Skinner's struggles to get his license to practice medicine in Paraguay and to get things going for the hospital, and then to witness firsthand the successful story of the hospital. Now the Baptist Hospital is a beautiful facility, well thought of in the city, region, and the nation. Today many doctors, nurses, and ancillary health providers train there.

Unlike our own country, there are seven doctors for every nurse in Paraguay. The hospital is aggressively training more nurses to fill the need.

Our large group was divided into teams. A bus took the team on which I served to our designated area, Union in the San Pedro area. We had to awaken at 5 a.m. to travel there, almost two hours away. We saw many patients that day and didn't return back to the hotel until 9:45 p.m.

The following day was filled with celebrations at the hospital. We met a lot of the staff and took a tour of the hospital. We then took a tour of the city via bus. Many police were spread all over the grounds of the Congressional Building. The government expected a demonstration at 5 p.m. protesting the then-current Paraguayan president. We visited the War Memorial Building also, including the grave of the unknown soldier.

That evening we had a celebration dinner at a large restaurant where Dr. Skinner and his family were honored. Most of his family were there for the celebration.

The following day my group went via bus to the local Baptist church in Arequa. There were crowds with lines twenty people thick. We were busy all day, especially the eye clinic, which was swamped and didn't finish up until 8:30 p.m. Peggy Bartley, retired IMB missionary to Uruguay, was my interpreter and helper in the clinic. She helped me do personal evangelism.

On August 7, 2002, my group went to a suburban church/school where Dr. Bryant and I did school physicals for approximately 400 children. The eye clinic was extremely busy again. At the end of the day as we were leaving it was so gratifying to see over 100 of the children lined up in the front of the school to bid us *adios*.

The next day our group went to Guarambare and worked in the local church. The eye clinic worked out under the trees where a large crowd was fitted for glasses. Occasionally, we would see a family or friends sipping mate together. That night the hotel staff put on a feast for us.

On August 9, 2002, a group of twenty-seven and I got up at 3 a.m. to leave by 4 a.m. for the Achee Indian trip. The Achee Indians are a very isolated group of people on a reserve in the rain forest of South Paraguay. They still hunt with bow and arrows and basically are a very primitive tribe. The government helps with their protection from the outside world. Unfortunately for us, it rained over three inches that night. We found out, while we ate breakfast at 3:30 a.m., that our trip had been canceled due to impassable, rain-soaked roads. We were quite disappointed as we had really looked forward to this portion of the trip, but God always knows best.

Later that morning, we joined the other groups and went to Paso Correro. There I drained a large axillary abscess that a local doctor hadn't done because the patient couldn't afford it.

We saw a large number of other patients that day and witnessed to many. Several accepted Jesus as Savior.

We returned to our hotel that evening and held clinic for the employees and their families. Peggy Sims, Dr. and Mrs. Bill Skinner's daughter, had been my interpreter all day, so I asked her to continue doing so at the hotel. She asked why we didn't go out in the line and witness to the people as they waited. I told her we could do it in our "clinic room" (TV room at the hotel). I soon figured out why I didn't get to go to the Achee Indian village. Peggy presented the plan of salvation to nine people, and out of this, four of the five that didn't know Jesus as Savior, accepted him. It was a very gratifying day.

On August 8 we rose early again and left by 5 a.m. for the

Jesuit ruins. We went to an old Jesuit church originally built in the 1700s. Now it was a museum showing and telling the history of the area. From there we went to the Mission which was built over a 50-year period in the first half of the 1700s. Some of the brick walls were still intact. I found it phenomenal what was built back then. The pulpit and baptismal were still intact. We then made it to Iguazu City to our hotel for the night.

The next morning we went to the Brazilian side of Iguazu Falls. This is the largest water falls in the world, fourteen times larger than Niagra Falls. The spectacular falls lie on the border between Brazil and Argentina and forms a part of the national parks in each country. The water falls consists of about 275 separate falls. The combined falls measure about two miles wide and drops 237 feet.

After seeing that waterfalls I can now appreciate more of the majesty, beauty, and grandeur of God's creation. The cascading water with a constant roar and the numerous falls beautified by a frequent display of rainbows in the mist were just magnificent. I wanted to take a ride in the river to get close to the falls, but that was nearly a day journey, not in the scope of our time limit.

Jonathan Bohn, Linda Coakley, and I went on a helicopter ride over the falls. From there we could see the whole panorama of the falls and the immense size all at once. In the distance, we could see the man-made dam which takes advantage of the force of water and gravity to produce electricity.

We briefly visited the point where Paraguay, Brazil, and Argentina all meet at one point. Then we headed back to Asuncion.

The next day we went shopping in downtown. I bought a few of the fine lace doilies and table runners that Paraguay is known for worldwide. Later that day, we returned to the airport for the flight home.

It was truly a great trip. I learned that a missionary and his family can do so much for a country and God. I admire the Skinners, Kents, and many others who have done so much for Paraguay and for the Lord there. I felt blessed by the trip and experience.

In 2004, I was invited to join a large group which went back to Asuncion to do more mission work through the Paraguay Baptist Foundation. That trip was scheduled June 27 through July 8. Al and Peggy Hethcock were the coordinators; Al and Marlin Harris were the team leaders. This was the same organization as the trip in 2002. The Baptist Hospital is well known locally and nationally for its superb treatment and care.

A group of 30 volunteers came from multiple places within the U.S. to serve on the two teams. We arrived in Asuncion after traveling all night from Dallas through Sao Paulo, Brazil. Shortly after arrival we went for a tour of the Baptist Hospital and met the Paraguay BMC Foundation president and several of the members of the the Foundation and hospital staff. I toured most of the facility in 2002 and again this time. I was impressed by what a nice facility they have. I know the people there are very proud of it. The hospital now is self-sustaining—that means it is no longer supported financially by the IMB. We then went back to the Portal del Sol Hotel, which is really a nice facility where one can get great food, lodging, and services.

Early on the morning of Tuesday, June 29, the *Amor* (Spanish for "love") team went with Marlin to the Consultorio Comunitario (Out Patient Community Clinic) to see patients while the *Esperanza* (Spanish for "hope") team went to Colonia Maka (Maka Village) to see patients. I was on the Amor team with Marlin. We saw several dozen people, and I was able to do more evangelizing that day than any other day of the trip. I remember fondly a father and 12-year-old son who accepted Jesus as Savior while using my Evangicube. I offered my dental capabilities (extracting teeth), but due to government bureaucracy like in Brazil and Venezuela that was not to be done in town.

On Wednesday, June 30, Amor went to Luque Genesaret at a local church while the Esperanza team went to the outpatient clinic at the hospital. Again Amor saw more than 200 medical patients.

On Thursday, July 1, Amor went to Chololo and Esperanza went to Yeguarizo, a small town outside of Acahey, situated 100 kilometers southeast of Asuncion. The Clyde E. Bay Foundation has a clinic there where missionaries and volunteers provide various services to the community. Our team saw over 200 patients and the eye team saw at least 100 more.

On Friday, July 2, we went to Lomita and Esperanza went to Limpio. Dr. Ben Ortellado is a doctor at the Baptist Hospital and is a pastor at Lomita where our team worked the whole day. It was a madhouse. We saw over 550 medical patients and at least 275 more eye patients. Marlin almost tired of me saying *proximo* (Spanish for "next"). We saw families of three to five members frequently. We joked that by the end of the day all our tongues were hanging out. We knew this would be a great drawing card for Dr. Ben, who would benefit from attention the church received that day.

On Saturday, July 3, Amor went to Nueva Italia and Esperanza went to Aregua Isla Valle. There was a huge crowd at Nueva Italia. The mayor had made announcements and the clinic had been advertised in the local newspaper. That day I got to be an exodontist (tooth extractor) with Evon, the dentist from the Baptist Hospital. She was impressed by my services and ability to pull teeth (almost painlessly), so she allowed me to pull teeth the next day at the same location by myself. She agreed to be on cell phone standby if I had a problem. I pulled fifty-five teeth Saturday and 110 on Sunday. Yes, Sunday! We were asked to work that day because of the total days we were to work fell that way. The Esperanza team joined us, and we really saw a lot of patients (medical, dental, and optical). Because it was July 4th, we met in the auditorium of the church and sang a couple of patriotic songs, including *God Bless America.*

Monday, July 5, we went to the Presidential Palace and met the first lady of Paraguay. Our group presented her with an English/Spanish Bible. She appeared to be quite appreciative. She asked us to pray for Paraguay as the country was in such a mess when her husband took over a year earlier. The President and First Lady of Paraguay are devout Christians. I hope you will join me in praying daily for Paraguay.

Our visit marked the first time ever a group of over ten was allowed into the Presidential Palace. Our group numbered over 40. The First Lady thanked us graciously for helping attend to the needs of the indigenous in her country. She asked us to return again soon. We were able to take a group picture with her, which we understand is not done very often.

Then we loaded up and headed back to Iguazu Falls along the Brazil-Argentina border. It was almost a five-hour drive to Brazil where we spent the night.

On Tuesday, July 6, we went via bus to cross into the Argentina side of the Falls. As we were going through customs Faith and Anon Schmidt's baby was not allowed to cross the border because she was only two months old and did not have her papers yet. The Schmidts left the bus and went back to our hotel. Due to the time factor and the incidence involving the Schmidts we decided to go back to the Brazil side to see the

Falls. The Schmidts joined us there. Actually, you can see more of the Falls from the Brazil side. We all enjoyed the beauty and magnificence of God's creation. Despite the constant roar of falling water in the distance, the area seemed so peaceful and serene. We did some souvenir shopping on the way back to the hotel.

On Wednesday, July 7, 2004, we held a clinic for hotel employees and their families for nearly three hours. Besides the hotel crowd our teams saw 2,756 medical patients, 1,488 eye patients, and eighty-six dental patients. The best part was that 352 people at the clinics (not counting the hotel crowd) accepted Jesus as Savior. To God be the Glory! It was a very good trip. My roommate was Dr. Buzz Jack, who is a retired surgeon and now a seminary student. We sure enjoyed evangelizing during the trip.

We were all very appreciative of our coordinators, Al and Peggy Hethcock, and the other team leader, Marlin Harris. I know Al and Peggy spent months organizing all the details of this trip.

Chapter 20

Return to Rio de Janeiro

August/September 2002

About five months prior to departure, Brenda Wisdom, R.N., contacted me about going back to Rio de Janiero. I had been there with Dr. Dewey Dunn and a group sponsored by the Tennessee Baptist Convention in November 2000. This was part of the state convention's five-year partnership with the Rio de Janeiro convention. Brenda asked me to help with the medical team. We were to work with Sharon Fairchild, IMB missionary to Brazil, as our group had done previously I had really enjoyed that trip and was anxious to go again.

Brenda called later and asked me to bring an Evangicube. She said Sharon Fairchild had been having great results using it with the groups moving into Rio de Janeiro. I just happened to have one that was given to me by Monica Wolfe who was on our Thailand mission trip. I had actually never put it to use.

Buddy and Rose Mary Andrews again graciously agreed to go with me. As we flew to Brazil I got out my Evangicube and read and re-read the instructions and Bible verses, many of which I was already very familiar. To me this is just the Gospel condensed on a Rubic cube.

We arrived at the Luxor Regente Hotel on the Copacobana Beach in Rio de Janeiro and immediately went to orientation led by Sharon Fairchild. Then we held a pill-counting and packing session to get ready for the next day of clinic. A few of us went out to the Projecto Espereranca and Igreja Batisa Transfiguracao (Portugese for the Spirit Project and Transfiguration Baptist Church) where we were to hold clinic that week. It was in an area called a *favella* (Portugese for slum area). We were told that we were to leave daily before night or we would be at risk for robbery.

The following morning we went via bus to the church and clinic site and started early to hold a full-day clinic. I met several people with whom I would be working for the next several years. The patients were given the Evangicube presentation in the church auditorium right after triage. This occurred again sometimes in the hallway while they waited to see a doctor or dentist. We doctors presented it again if they hadn't by then accepted Jesus as Savior.

Nilton de Silva was my interpreter the first day. Nilton translated my first-ever Evangicube presentation, which resulted in people accepting Jesus as Savior. That was a thrill that was repeated many times that week.

The next day was Sunday so we attended church at the Igreja Batista Transfiguracao. The pastor there introduced our group and several of our members sang a couple of songs. Brenda, Dr. Biddle and I presented our testimonies.

After church we went to McDonalds for lunch, then drove to the "Hippie Fair" or open market on Copacobana Beach to buy some souvenirs.

The following day we started clinic again. Karen Gray, IMB missionary to Brazil, was my interpreter. We saw many patients that day, but I was more excited about presenting the Gospel via the Evangicube to all who did not have Jesus in their hearts. Several accepted Jesus. Karen seemed just excited as I was about all the new believers.

Occasionally we would experience a break in the line of patients. I would go see the other team members seeing patients. Rose Mary and Buddy were working in the dental clinic with our dentists, Dale and Fred. Charles Manley and Trenton Wallace were in the pharmacy. The eye clinic was always busy. Nancy Newman, nurse practitioner, and Dr. Michael Biddle, my roommate, were working in pediatrics.

At night we all looked forward to eating out in a Beach area restaurant. One night I went with a couple of the doctors to an Italian restaurant on Ipanema Beach. We had goose liver for an appetizer before the main course.

One morning on the way to the clinic we came across a man lying in the street, He had been hit by a bus. People on the bus, recognizing that I was a medical doctor, asked me to look after him. I quickly obtained some gloves and went to see him. He was not breathing and blood was pouring from a head wound. I quickly opened his airway and he started to breath. Someone else put pressure on his head wound to control the bleeding. Our missionary on the bus called the police for an ambulance (which was two blocks away). After ten minutes the ambulance finally arrived. By that time the man was starting to arouse and the bleeding had subsided. We then proceeded to the clinic.

A photographer kept taking pictures of us frequently. Finally we determined that where two or more Baptists gathered this photographer would be there. Actually, he did take some good photographs. so I ended up buying six of them.

One day a young lady came in with a large chronic ulcer on her leg. When I pulled off the bandage, blood went everywhere. April, nurse practitioner, and Brenda left rapidly and so did all the patients; I was left holding the leg until the bleeding subsided so I could get some new dressings. She needed a skin graft for the large, open, granulating wound, so we recommended that she go to the hospital for this.

Another day before noon I was asked to see a patient at her home two miles from the clinic being held in a church. One of the missionaries drove me during the lunch break to see the elderly lady. I could find no particular ailment other than age and debility, so I gave her some pain pills and multiple vitamins. She and her family were so gracious and happy that we came out to see them.

We did not always see just the usual things. A young girl came to see us with a cold but more importantly she had Riser Syndrome (skull deformities and syndactyl of her fingers). She was to have skull surgery soon, so we treated her for the cold.

At the end of the clinic, we had a meeting or party for and gave gifts to all the Brazilian staff who helped us in the clinic. They were so appreciative. We had a big celebration cake following the gifts. The pastor stated that clinics like this really helped his church enrollment. No wonder, during the week we saw a total of 1,768 patients (230 dentistry, 532 adult medical, 442 pediatrics, 604 in the eye clinic) and filled 2,784 prescriptions. Out of this group 349 accepted Jesus as Savior. To God be the glory! That night we celebrated further by going to the Hard Rock Cafe for dinner. A few of our "sinful Baptists" even line danced.

The next day our group went on a harbor (bay) cruise, but that did not impede our evangelistic efforts. Our guide, and later the captain and first mate, were led to the Lord through our Gospel presentations. After lunch we went to Sugar Loaf Mountain in the bay and rode the cable car to the top. Looking out over the city and Copacobana Beach it is easy to understand why Rio de Janeiro is called "the beautiful city".

During that day, one of our team members even led our bus driver to Jesus by using the Evangicube.

This trip was memorable in many ways, but mainly for how I learned to evangelize with the Evangicube. I have found that the Evangicube is just about the most useful tool that I have ever used to share the Gospel and love of Jesus. I admire all the IMB missionaries to Brazil who are doing a great work there for the Lord.

CHAPTER 21

North Benin West Africa

November 2002

After I performed that appendectomy on Suzanne Crocker in June 2001, she and husband John, had invited me to return to Africa and serve with them at some point. Dr. Richard Thomassian of T.I.M.E. Ministries (Training in Ministerial Evangelism) had already planned a trip to Natitingou and north Benin for some time to work in the Crockers' missionary territory. His trip turned out to be God's way of returning me to west Africa to minister alongside the Crockers.

The Crockers are originally from Whitesburg Baptist Church in Huntsville, Alabama, They had been in Togo and north Benin for as least eight years.

Dr. Thomassian ("Bro. Dick") and his secretary, Beverly Dishman, contacted me after I had already planned to go to north Benin to serve with John and Suzanne. He asked me to coordinate the medical team. Bro. Dick already had the evangelism team trained and ready to go.

As usual, it was difficult to recruit physicians for the trip. When I invited Dr. Larry Daniels, who worked at the DeSoto Regional Health System (hospital) in Mansfield, Louisiana, as an agency emergency-room physician, to go to north Benin with us, I saw a sparkle in his eyes that didn't fade. He said he would love to go, but wanted to pray about it first and see if he could get the time off from his work. He added that he had always wanted to go to Africa to trace his roots. I told him we would look under every tree in west Africa to find his roots if he would go with us. Later he told me he would go.

I also had become more acquainted with T.I.M.E. Ministries. It was started a few years ago by Dr. Thomassian and his uncle. Thanks to their diligent work it had flourished in its ministry to several countries all over the world. Its purpose was to take the Gospel through dramas, puppets, and good ole evangelistic preaching to all that would listen.

Beverly had sent me a picture of Bro. Dick so I could recognize him at the Atlanta airport. He and his wife, Lois, were walking down the corridor toward our gate of departure. While waiting to depart to Paris, we had a delightful conversation about his ministry and the Crockers.

After a tiring flight, we finally made it to Cotonou, Benin. We were glad to make it to our hotel. Many of the evangelical team stayed at the Baptist Guest House in the city.

The following morning the medical team went with the evangelical team to the Fidjrosee Baptist Church in Cotonou for a series of dramas and evangelism. After the evangelistic message by Bro. Dick, many accepted Jesus as Savior. Immediately afterward everyone went to a place not far from the church into an opening near a school, and the program was presented to a large crowd that had assembled. Again many accepted Jesus as Savior.

Sunday morning everyone went to the Vodje Baptist Church near the beach in Cotonou. The evangelical presentation was given again. Many accepted Jesus as Savior. After lunch we went to an opening on the beach near an open market and presented the program again. As before, many accepted the Lord as Savior. Immediately following that, the group went to the outskirts of the city for further presentation of the Gospel. By this time, it was completely dark, but under the lights provided by a generator, the program and Gospel were presented again; and again many accepted the Lord as Savior.

The next morning we packed our gear and medical supplies and drove north to Parakou, situated about the middle of Benin, and spent the night in a hotel. The Crockers met us at the hotel early the next morning. John took the evangelical team out in the city to do its thing while the medical team went with Suzanne to the edge of the city where a small thatched Baptist church had been started. We held clinic there for four hours.

Using the Evangicube, I led the first three patients to accept Jesus as Savior. One of these was an older Tamberma woman who had a wooden disk through her lower lip. After treatment, I asked her if she was a believer. She responded, "How can I be if no one had ever told me the way?" We shared the Gospel with her using the Evangicube. When we got to the picture of Christ on the cross, she clapped her hand over her mouth and made sounds of disbelief and horror. When she saw the picture of Christ raised from the tomb, she began to clap. At the end, she prayed to receive Christ. Then she asked a very important question, "When you leave who will teach me how to continue walking in the way?" We were delighted to tell her that a new Baptist church was meeting every Sunday at 7 a.m. in the building where we were holding our clinic. She was thrilled and replied, "I live close by. I can come."

The village chief then came and told Suzanne we would never see all the patients at the rate we were going, so I abandoned my personal evangelism and gave the Evangicube to the pastor's wife who then made good use of it leading more to Jesus.

We saw some patients with malaria, pulled a few teeth, and wrapped up the clinic. Since I didn't get to do personal evangelism, I felt led to talk with the people remaining in the clinic area. I had them gather under a large tree nearby and presented the Gospel and plan of salvation as best I could in a few minutes. Twenty-three accepted Jesus.

Afterwards our entire group drove to Natitingou to our hotel which would be our lodging for the next four nights. The Hotel Tata Somba was very nice and had very good food.

The following morning the evangelistic team went its way and ministered to schools, prisons, and at the market place, and then to the soccer stadium that night and every night while we were there. It turned out to be "a great reaping of the harvest" as several hundred accepted Jesus as Savior during these endeavors.

Meanwhile, the medical team went on to Boukambe, less than a mile from the border with Togo, the nation west of Benin. We went to the medical center in the center of the city. No doctors—just four nurses with limited medical and pharmaceutical supplies—were in the area. The crowd was large and waited under partial shade in front of the clinic as the day proceeded to get hotter and hotter.

Initially we saw all the patients from the back door until we realized they were all relatives and friends of the nurses, so I insisted we see the people out front. Progressively the crowd became unruly, with people pushing in line and crowding in very closely. Finally, I told Suzanne to tell them we were leaving immediately if they didn't behave.

We were able to see several patients. I even excised a large lipoma from a lady's thigh. If we hadn't been there she would have had to go 200 miles to have the procedure done. Incidentally, during all of this Sarah Joy, the Crockers' oldest daughter, was under the table sleeping from sedation I had given her for vomiting.

One man told us he had walked 30 miles to get there after he heard he could get free medical treatment from doctors.

Dr. Daniels was next door seeing pediatric patients. There was no way we could see every one that day because of such a large crowd. We were forced to get home by dark because the roads are shut down at night.

Boukambe has no Baptist church, but John hoped to get one started soon.

The next day we went to Kausso Kaingu medical clinic, about six miles from Boukambe. Again no doctors and few medical supplies were present. The chief of this village had heard about our troubles at Boukambe and assured us of proper crowd control. The crowd was quiet all day. We worked all day and saw many people, pulled several teeth, and even did a little minor surgery. We got back to Natitingou just as officials were closing down the road for the night.

The following day, November 8, 2002, we held clinic at John and Suzanne's house in Natitingou. We had patients all day and extracted several teeth. I even did a circumcision on one child who had severe phimosis. We used Chris Crocker's baby bed to operate on as that was the only place we had to lay the patient. When Chris came in and saw us using his bed as an operating table, you should have heard him scream.

The most memorable event that day (and the whole trip) was when I got to meet the Mother Teresa of Africa—or better called Mamma Phoebe of Africa. Phoebe is an ordained minister for the Assembly of God church in Natitingou; her husband also is a minister. Phoebe and her husband have an orphanage with several children. They have little money to feed the children, but she said the Lord always provides. She had brought in four or five of her children from the orphanage. She was suckling (breast feeding) a set of orphan twins. Keep in mind is 50 years old; this was a true miracle of God. Suzanne told me Phoebe had prayed to be able to lactate so the children would not starve. (She had been doing this for several children over the years.) She truly loves her people.

I was so busy seeing patients, with Suzanne interpreting for me, that I didn't have time to evangelize with my Evangicube. So I explained it to Phoebe, and she went out in the line of patients and with it led 30 people to the Lord in one hour. She was so excited she came and got Suzanne and they went in the next room to pray and thank God for the conversions.

Phoebe is truly an amazing person. John Crocker said she was also the best female preacher he had ever heard. At the end of the clinic, I asked her if these new converts were going to be Baptists or Assembly of God people. She said, "Baptist, there is enough here to go around for everyone."

After the clinic, Suzanne took us to the nearby Ardet-Atacara Falls; it was beautiful. Suzanne, Laverne (our "pharmacist" for the week and tutor to the Crocker children, as provided by the IMB), went wading in the river along with Dr. Larry.

The crusade ended that night with more harvesting of souls. Dr. Thomassian and the T.I.M.E. Ministries arranged to donate enough funds to build a Baptist church in downtown Natitingou. (Later a gentleman donated enough land on which to build the church.)

The next day we drove 10 hours back to Cotonou, a long

hard drive, especially for Bro. Dick who, by this time, was having rather severe back pain. I had injected his back with steroids, but it didn't help much.

The following day we met the Hoffmans; Alice is a former member of Whitesburg Baptist Church. The Hoffmans supervise a large mission ship that goes from port to port all over the world evangelizing to large numbers on and off the ship.

That night we flew from Cotonou to Paris; then to Atlanta and back home. It was truly a memorable trip. Dr. Larry and I promised to return again the next year, this time to Kare, Togo, where the Crockers reside.

CHAPTER 22

Nicaragua

January 2003

During the trip to Guatemala in 2002 I kept asking Marie Agee, coordinator for Health Talents International, about the annual Nicaragua trip they make to Managua every year. She invited me to go on that trip; it was a medical trip, not a surgical one like Guatemala which I had made for the last four years. Therefore, I arranged to go with the group and put off my annual trip to Guatemala until April 2003.

A medical team of fourteen traveled through Houston to Managua on January 23, 2003; we made it to our hotel (Hotel Las Cabanas) late that night. The next morning at breakfast I became acquainted with all the members of the team I had not met on the way to Managua. Then we proceeded to go to the Rene Polaco Church where we would hold clinic for the next two days.

Gary Tabor borrowed my dental tools and started to pull teeth when a Nicaraguan oral surgeon and two other dentists who were in training showed up to help. The dental work was turned over to them, with Gary assisting and cleaning the instruments. I worked in the medical section with Dr. Charles Jarret, internist, Dr. Alan Boyd, dermatologist, and Dr. David Weed, pediatrician. We worked in the outpatient clinic at the church where people in the church and community are seen on a scheduled basis. Dr. Nauendis and Dr. Mena, native Nicaraguans who worked in the clinic there, came to help our group with the large crowd that had gathered to be seen.

The following day, Saturday, a large crowd of children showed up for the breakfast program. This program has been a great success as it has been a method to attract people to the church. After the children get involved, the parents get involved too. The program feeds poor children in Rene Polanco Church and the community, and follows up on the children's growth. A doctor sees them regularly, and advises them and their mothers in personal health care. The Medical Missions Ministry at Waterview Church of Christ in Richardson, Texas, supports the breakfast program of the medical clinic at Rene Polanco. The clinic furnishes breakfast three times a month on Saturdays for the church and neighborhood children. The breakfast consists of juice, milk, cereal, bread, and eggs. Women of the congregation prepare the food. After breakfast Bible lessons are conducted.

The Rene Polanco Clinic has an evangelistic program which supports a preacher so that he can preach the Gospel in the clinic facilities during the medical services. An eyeglasses program benefits both church members and non-church members in the area. Grace McIntyre headed up the eye clinic. A small laboratory is available at the clinic. As part of an Integral Health Program, the clinic led the building of three houses for poor widows who are members of Rene Polanco Church. A dental clinic was being planned for the clinic soon. Taking care of the people's physical needs attracts them for their spiritual needs.

Pastor Jerry Ervin, who has been on the trip to Guatemala several times, gave our spiritual message Sunday morning at the church/clinic. After church, we went out to the Children's Program site where they have another Breakfast Program.

Following that we went downtown to the market place to buy a few souvenirs, then we proceeded to go out to the Mombacho Volcano Park where there is a large inactive crater. In the distance from the summit of the crater you can see Lake Nicaragua. That night we watched part of the Super Bowl which was on TV at the hotel.

Clouds of acrid smoke, dust, and buzzards were everywhere at the city dump. Another garbage truck would arrive and immediately a dozen or more people would descend on the waste as it was poured on the ground, sorting anything of value. If it was edible, they ate it. Scraps of anything metal or plastic were sorted into individual piles to be sold. The remainder was consumed by the buzzards or it was tossed onto one of the many smoldering heaps of refuse deemed to be of no value. The cows ate anything that was vegetable. Dwelling sites were everywhere on the periphery of the dump, mostly made out of cardboard and scavenged wood. Such was the scene we saw prior to going to clinic that morning to show how some of the poor live in Managua.

We proceeded to hold a clinic at the Church of Christ near the dump. The demand for medical attention was so great we began to run out of medication in the middle of the afternoon. Intestinal parasites, as you would expect, were rampant. Lice and scabies were prevalent. We frequently saw rashes, fungal and bacterial infections, as well as the usual respiratory infections. Aches and pains were the main adult complaint. The people were appreciative of their treatment and medications.

For the three days of clinics in Managua, the team saw and ministered to 1,485 Nicaraguans with medical care, dental work, new glasses, and 6,000 prescriptions. It was a great trip to see how caring Health Talents International is for the people and the spiritual aid they minister to the people of Nicaragua. The team was a joy with which to work.

Chapter 23

Jamaica

July 2003

As promised, Dr. Larry Daniels and I were making plans to go to Togo to serve with John and Suzanne Crocker. Despite her being about twenty-three weeks pregnant, Suzanne had emailed me and said she still wanted us to come anyway. I had ordered medications and airplane tickets were ready to be ordered when I got the news that Suzanne was being flown home to Huntsville, Alabama, because she had gone into premature labor. Our trip was cancelled, but we were invited to go with Dr. Richard Thomassian to the T.I.M.E's evangelical crusade to Jamaica in mid July.

I was asked to head the medical team like I did in north Benin when the T.I.M.E. Ministries went there for a weeklong crusade. I had to call Blessings International and CrossLink International and ask permission to take the medicines and supplies I had ordered from them to take to a different country. They graciously agreed as long as I was using them for a mission trip in a foreign land. I was sent new certificates for the meds and supplies from Blessings International and CrossLinks International to take to Jamaica.

I was able to recruit some faithful and reliable friends for the trip: my wife, Vickie, and Rose Mary and Buddy Andrews. Dr. J.D. Turner was invited to go on the trip also and several members of the T.I.M.E. team later helped us out in the clinics while in Jamaica. A total of 15 team members were assigned to the medical teams. Beverly Dishman, Dr. Thomassian's secretary, coordinated our flights to Jamaica

On arriving in Montego Bay we were serenaded by a group of singers at the airport. After settling in at Gloriana Hotel all of our group went with the evangelistic team to the Montego Bay downtown square to hold an evangelistic presentation. The puppet show, several dramas by the evangelical team, singing, and good old evangelistic preaching by Dr. Thomassian (Bro.Dick) occurred. Several people raised their hands giving an indication that they had received Jesus into their heart.

The next day was Sunday so we went to the Westgate Church, present home church of Dr. Heckford Sharpe; he is the pastor there. We were asked to give testimonies, sing, and one of our group even played a trumpet.

The next day our two medical teams were taken by bus to our assigned places. My team was sent to the Barnett Baptist Church which is in downtown Montego Bay; it is also his office site. It is located over Mikey's Cash-N-Carry, a convenience store. The first day we saw several people there for routine complaints and illnesses. I got permission from Dr. Sharpe to also pull teeth, but he was a little hesitant at first. He had a dental room with two real dental chairs, but the room was stifling hot as it had no air conditioning or even a fan. I seemed almost punished in that room to be pulling teeth, but it was so nice to have a real dental chair for a change.

Dr. Turner and his team went to the Webster Baptist Church across the bay; we rode the bus with his group prior to being taken to our location.

Every morning and every night we had very delicious

meals prepared for us by the ladies from Whitesburg Baptist Church in Huntsville, Alabama. They daily prepared sandwiches for us to take on our excursions to our various clinic sites.

We worked at the Barnett Baptist Church for five days. It was surprising how many people had hypertension. Buddy and Rose Mary worked at the spiritual station using the Evangicube. Some ladies from Whitesburg Baptist also helped out there also. I was kept busy seeing patients and pulling teeth. One day people from the Tampa Bay Church came in and helped out with registration, witnessing, and at the other stations.

Each day driving the other team out to their work site we could see the large hospital, Cornwall Regional Medical Center.

While shopping late one evening I bought a hat that had dreadlocks. I wore this to clinic the next morning. Dr. Sharpe thought it was hilarious and insisted I take a picture of him wearing the dreadlocks.

One afternoon we saw the evangelism team down the street presenting their dramas, showing their puppets, and Bro. Dick preaching.

On the evening of July 25, 2004, we went to the Westgate Baptist Church and saw Dr. Heckford Sharpe's dream. He has the vision of building a church to seat 4,000 behind their present location. It has a fair amount of construction done, but at the rate it is being built, it will take years. The cost of material and labor is such a problem at present. The construction team that went with the T.I.M.E. Ministries had worked about ten hours every day. They had poured concrete on the second floor of one side of the present structure, but it almost seemed small compared to what all needed to be done to finish the project.

T.I.M.E. Ministries paid for several thousand dollars of materials.

That evening we had a block party in front of the Westgate Church. Food was prepared for the large number of people that came. Several of Vickie's students in Vacation Bible School week came to give greetings to her. I photographed most of them. Bro. Dick got to have one more service that night, then our group leaders were presented plagues or clocks thanking them for working in Montego Bay that week.

During the week the medical team led 33 to accept Christ. The evangelistic team had very good results along with the Vacation Bible Schools July 21 to July 25.

The total number of salvation decisions for the week reached 1,089. As Bro Dick said, "To God be the glory, great things he hath done." It had been a good week. We went home the next day.

CHAPTER 24

Burkina Faso

January 2004

An invitation to go on a medical mission to Burkina Faso arrived by mail from Stephanie Ragland of Healthcare Volunteers in the Volunteers in Missions Department at the IMB. This request came from Rev. Jeff Hickman and Rev. Jamie Arnette of Mt. Calvary Baptist in Dillon, South Carolina. They had researched this mission-field region (Burkina Faso) in 2002 and found little or no volunteers going to this area.

The IMB missionary in Burkina Faso, Lynn Kennedy, told the group at Mt. Calvary in Dillon to make sure they enlisted as many people as possible to pray for the team effort and mission trip scheduled to come there. She said they did not want casual prayer partners, but instead desired dedicated prayer warriors. Rev. Hickman had relayed the message that spiritual warfare was being fought there and the group must be prepared. He further explained that the region is under the control of witch doctors and root doctors. Spiritism is the main religious focus of many people there. Satan knows what a tremendous impact our teams make on this area of the world and he will try to stop us at any cost from going. Rev. Hickman further emphasized how we should prepare spiritually for this trip.

The request went out for three groups with three to five teams each with two or more doctors per team. The dates for the first group were January 9-18. For the second group the dates were January 30-February 8. A small team was slated to go for approximately two weeks later in February. Lynn Kennedy said, "This would be the first medical mission to this region where the Dagaari people reside."

After agreeing to go I recruited Paulette Holt, R.N. from McLeod, Texas; she works in the ER where I work about once weekly at North Caddo Medical Center. Later I saw on the volunteer list that Ann McConathy from Haughton, La. was going; she only lives 10 miles from my home, and I had never met her (strange that we would meet on the way to the other side of the world).

All communications were done by email or telephone with Rev. Jamie Arnette, our coordinator; Rev Hickman had just been "called" to another church. I told Jamie I would order meds from Blessings International, CrossLinks International, and M.A.P. International. I also wrote Alcon Labs and got them to donate dozens of their eye drops/ointments for our mission trip. I had most of this shipped to Dillon, S.C., so it could be taken to Burkina Faso by members of the group from there as their second suitcase.

After meeting the group of twelve at the Atlanta airport, we boarded an Air France airplane and flew to Paris overnight, then on to Ouagadougou, capital city of Burkina Faso.

We met Lynn Kennedy and Sean Miller, a two-year Journeyman, at the airport in Ouagadougou and spent the night at the Baptist Mission House.

The next day was Sunday so we all went to the Baptist Church in Ouagadougou. We were introduced at the church as short-term missionaries from America and stood at the front of the church and shook hands with the members of the church. We were well received and the people seemed to really appreciate that we came all the way to Burkina Faso to minister to the people there. Immediately afterwards we took off southwest for a four-hour drive to our area of work. Along the way we saw the true nature of the countryside—dry, dusty, and rocky. The weather was hot because the nation is sub-Sahara or a tropical climate. Two distinct seasons exist there: dry and rainy. We were there for the dry season in January. Lynn told us it gets to 120 degrees at times. Most of the streams were almost dry, but we observed one bridge that was washed out during the last rainy season being repaired. Cotton fields often fill the horizon, but now had all been completely picked to the last boll.

Team 1 was left at a village named Kammabou. This team of two doctors, two nurses, an ordained minister, and two laymen stayed in the village all week—out in the middle of nowhere. Initially they seemed a little skeptical about this, especially since there were no telephones, no running water, no electricity, and they were unfamiliar with the people there.

Our team consisted of Sean (the Journeyman), Rev. Jamie Arnette (the coordinator of our trip), Paulette Holt, Chris Chambers, and me. We went to Sean's missionary house, one hour's drive further south. The missionary residence was comfortable, but it had no running water. Its electricity came from a system of solar panels and storage batteries. After arrival we had almost all the lights and fans on, then everything went dark. We had exhausted the batteries before we expected. This taught us immediately to conserve on energy use. Until recently the house had been occupied by a married couple serving as missionaries there, but Sean lived in the large house by himself.

The next morning we loaded up our meds and supplies in Sean's truck and went a few miles to our first village. Along the way we noted that all the houses and even schools were made of mud-bricks and most had nearly flat roofs. The main road was being constructed by French contractors who were laying asphalt. Sean told us this would be a major route to do commerce with Ghana, which was several more miles to the west. As we came to the village of Tabieton we drove through a cotton-and-millet field to a large complex made of mud-bricks that was the main home for most of the villagers. Sean told us that when a new house is needed for more members of the family, it is joined onto the big complex. To me it looked like a medium-sized fort. In the distance we could see people going about their daily chores of feeding the animals, drawing water from a well, and watching children play.

The people had already begun to gather before we arrived. Sean and the local pastors had told the people of our team's plan to give a free medical clinic. The spiritual station was the first station that the people came to after registration. It was staffed by trained national ministers. Here the Gospel was given in the native tongue. Several people seemed touched by the message they were hearing.

Under a large mango tree near the housing complex we saw 144 patients and treated them for a variety of maladies. Many had long-standing ulcers on their legs that would not heal because of the dust everywhere, general lack of clean water, and no bandage materials. Paulette stayed busy much of her time cleansing and dressing wounds. I extracted ten teeth, but in general found their dental hygiene to be very good because they have little or no sugar in their diets. Almost everyone of the young children had *kwashiorkor* (malnutrition) as evidenced by their protruding abdomen and the universal presence of an umbilical hernia, many being quite prominent. The children apparently did not get enough protein in their diet causing the state of malnutrition. The older children or teenagers apparently got better nutrition as most of the protruding abdomens and umbilical hernias had nearly vanished.

The sunlight filtered through the mango tree as the sun went from east to west. It had blistered my forehead by noon, so I had to put my hat on for the remainder of the day. At the end of the day the village chief brought us a live chicken and two large *nyai* (yams) in appreciation for our visiting their village. We accepted them graciously as this was a real sacrifice on their part.

The next day we returned to Tabieton and saw 158 patients. I kept Jamie and Chris, who were running the pharmacy, busy all day. My challenge for the day was leading a Satan worshiper to accept Jesus Christ as Savior. I used the Evangicube as a pictorial method of the plan of salvation. According to Sean the new convert was undergoing the *Bowr* (Dagaari for initiation into being a Satan worshiper). He wore a bright red hat, bright clothes, and multiple bronze bracelets. One of my highlights for the week was showing this man that my God is greater than his god and witnessing his becoming a Jesus worshiper rather then a Satan worshiper.

A young woman presented a large, firm mass on her posterior right arm; I told her she needed to go to the hospital to have it excised. Sean told me if I didn't do it then, it would never get done. At the end of the day after seeing other patients I had Jamie and Chris clear the pickup truck of our meds and used it for an operating table. I anesthetized the arm with 30 cc of 1% Xylocaine with epinephrine and after prepping and draping it for surgery, the lady started groaning and became scared. This was most likely due to all the epinephrine in the Xylocaine solution as it can cause a sense of doom. I had to let her hold her baby in her left arm and her mother stand nearby while I operated on the right arm. The tumor dissected out very smoothly with no invasion of adjacent tissues. She seemed very grateful to have the mass off.

Every evening after clinic in the villages with the local Dagaari people we would have a time of sharing including prayer, song, testimonies, and scripture reading. While we were in the village of Tabieton, one of the village leaders who had been a Christian for about five years gave his testimony. He had been a Satan worshiper like so many of the Dagaari people. He used crutches because of affliction with polio when he was a young child. A small man in stature, but with a faith that would move mountains, he gave his testimony saying if you don't follow Jesus, you are cursed. The head Satan worshiper told him if he became a Christian, he would be dead in two weeks. He laughed when telling us this, and said, "I have been a Christian for five years. I no longer have to sacrifice and go through the Satan rituals. Now I eat the chickens that I once had to kill and give to Satan." His testimony, which was so humble and enlightening, was a true blessing to our team members and the crowd that was assembled there.

That night Sean, Chris, Jamie, and I drove an hour to Kammabou to check on the team there. They seemed quite happy and content despite no electricity or running water. The village people had made them an outdoor toilet (I'm sure much to the delight of the women on the team).

Meanwhile Paulette had cooked supper for us by the time we returned.

The next day we drove through a cotton field off the main road to Malko village to a "church" made out of a wooden frame with millet stalks forming the top and sides. Amazingly it was shaded and fairly cool inside, despite the 95 degrees heat outside, but the dust and humidity remained. We saw 160 patients, extracted ten teeth, did two field circumcisions on two one-year olds with severe phimosis. We saw a very ill ten-month-old baby who had volume depletion from vomiting and diarrhea. We tried to give some rehydration fluid but the baby promptly vomited twice, so I got Sean and Paulette to drive the mother and baby to the Diabougou hospital about 15 miles away. Paulette and I agreed to pay the hospital as the parents couldn't afford it. This required upfront money for the IV fluids, tubing, and starter kit, because medications had to be purchased before admission to the hospital. The baby was the son of the Satan worshiper who had accepted the Lord the previous day.

At the end of the day I again used our pickup truck as our operating table. Paulette helped me excise a large lipoma from the posterior chest wall of a young man. The village people offered us supper, but we graciously declined.

The following day we returned to Malko village and saw as many patients as possible. We even saw a couple of people from Ghana, which was more than 15 miles away. They somehow had found out we had a free medical clinic set up there. We saw 172 patients, extracted a few teeth, and did a third field circumcision. There were just too many people to be seen that day. I used my Evangicube to lead two more Satan worshippers to the Lord. Paulette borrowed my Evangicube and led another Satan worshiper to accept Jesus as Savior.

By the end of the day we had run out of vitamins, pain relievers, and several of the commonly used medications. By the second day we had used up all of our bandage materials and had to purchase more. Paulette kept busy cleansing and dressing wounds which couldn't heal because of the dust everywhere. We finally ran out of registration cards. Jamie said that was a definite stopping point.

Food was brought to us out of gratitude for our services. Only Sean braved eating the food. He said, "You have American stomachs, so don't try this unless you really want to." He later claimed that he had eaten their food for almost two years and had never been ill from it.

The people were so appreciative of our services. They invited us back again and asked if we or another group would be back soon. I commended them on their discipline. I've never seen a better controlled crowd anywhere in the world.

The following morning, January 16, we went by the home of Gawoso, my interpreter for the week, to see his father for symptoms of hypertension. Indeed he had a blood pressure of 210/110. We gave him the blood pressure meds we had left. We also treated a couple of Gawoso's children. Then we went back to Tabieton to check on our surgical patients. They were doing well. Then we went to the hospital in Diebougouto to check on the baby we had sent there. The baby was doing quite well and was to be discharged later that day. Paulette and I paid the hospital and doctor bills, a total of $38. (I had expected a bill of $200 or more.)

We drove to Kammabou to pick up team 1. Team 3 also met us there. By all reports everyone had a very good week ministering and working with the people.

We had a celebration time with the people during which it sprinkled rain for a couple of minutes. Lynn said, "To these people this was a very favorable sign from heaven for a job well done. It usually doesn't rain in Burkina Faso in January."

We then drove back to Ouagadougou to the mission house to spend the night. The next morning we went to the *marche* (local market). We were amazed how we were haggled by vendors who followed us up to two blocks down the street before they were finally convinced we were not going to buy their merchandise. I did buy a very ornamental knife from one of the Toureg people (Sahara desert nomads). That night we ate supper at one of the best restaurants in town, and everyone in our group got to share some of their experiences during the week.

During that week Lynn had shared with us how she had gone to seminary after her husband had died. She had wanted to be a missionary for many years. She told us that she researched the Dagaari people and chose to come to Burkina Faso. She related the fact that she had learned to love the people there. She plans to stay there until she dies.

Late that night we headed for the airport for the long journey back home.

CHAPTER 25

Honduras

April 2004

Once again Dr. Charles Walker called on me to help with some LSU medical students. He had been in contact with Randy Pierce, who runs a mission group called xMa (Extreme Missionary Adventures). Randy lives in Rayville, Louisiana, but groups from all over the U.S. go on trips he sets up, especially to Honduras. Charles made arrangements for med students of the LSU Baptist Student Union to go on a trip to Olanchito, Honduras, during their spring break.

A few days before we departed, Charles' father-in-law had surgery for a ruptured abdominal aortic aneurysm and was not doing well. He felt obligated to stay home, but he asked Dr. John Felty and me to guide and proctor the group of students. Charles rode with us to the New Orleans Airport, then returned in my car to Shreveport. (Charles' father-in-law died a few days later).

Our group flew from New Orleans on April 3rd to San Pedro Sula, then on to La Ceida which is not far from the Gulf of Mexico. We were met at the airport by Wally and the xMa group, who drove us to the mission house near Olanchito. The mission house is quite a charming place several miles from Olanchito off a deeply rutted road and situated in a quiet, serene setting next to a small river with mountains on both sides.

We all went to worship Sunday morning at Pastor Dario Delarca's church. Later that afternoon we chose teams. Most of the students wanted to hike up into the mountains, but a few decided to stay and work with me in the villages and Pastor Delarca's church. We spent part of the afternoon packing meds and supplies for the clinics the next day. That night we returned to the church and watched the *Passion of the Christ*. Many of the church members were quite moved by the movie. All of our group had already seen the movie.

Monday morning we all went to El Plan village at the base of the mountains. The trekkers took off with their backpacks into the mountains to minister and treat the people there as best possible.

My group stayed in El Plan village and saw multiple illnesses. I started pulling teeth and was soon overwhelmed with necrotic teeth. The villagers must have found out an *el dentista* was in the village. I pulled ten teeth from one person. My interpreter said the people failed to brush their teeth.

We left each person with a toothbrush and toothpaste. The students really enjoyed the freedom to see and treat the people. I was their consultant for any questions.

The mountain group later told us they made it mostly by four-wheel-drive trucks. They spent the night with some bed partners in the form of scorpions.

Tuesday my group went to the village of Chapparal and saw many patients. I pulled several teeth while out under a mango tree. Pastor Dario held our spiritual station. Occasionally he would ask me to use the Evangicube to visually show the Gospel or for a difficult case. One such case was his nephew. The young man called it the "Magic Cube". No one I presented it to refused to accept Jesus as Savior. The trekkers came home that evening with many stories about their adventures in the mountains.

Wednesday my group went to La Evidia (New Sanai) where a new church was being built. We had clinic in the backyard of one of Pastor Dario's friends. I helped the students see more than fifty patients and was a frequent consultant to them for any questions. I pulled several teeth also.

Thursday our team went to Asilio de Ancious, a nursing home, and treated ten people. Then we went to Pastor Dario's church to see and treat people. For lunch we went to Pastor Dario's home a few blocks away. The native Honduran food was very good. After lunch the students continued to see a large number of patients. When not consulting with the students, I continued to extract teeth and do some minor surgery.

The trekkers returned after dark telling us of further adventures: seeing a lot of patients, evangelizing, and seeing beautiful country. They were extremely happy about their trip into the mountains.

Friday we relaxed at the mission house. Several including me went swimming and riding inner tubes down the river. That afternoon after a cookout at the mission house, most of us went hammock shopping. Then the group went shopping for carved-wood items. That evening we packed to go home.

One of the Honduran workers tried passionately to learn English. Instead of buying more souvenirs which I really didn't need, I talked with Pastor Dario and donated some money for the woman to take English classes.

Early Saturday at 3:40 a.m., we all got up to begin the trip back to the U.S. We had to drive back to La Ceiba for our flight scheduled at 8:30 a.m. I had been riding with Marlin Reyes, Pastor Dario's nephew, all week so I again chose to ride in his vehicle to the airport. I got in the back seat so I could nap on the trip. Just west of Olanchito on a smooth asphalt road Marlin bent down to get a cassette tape off the floor. He briefly lost sight of the road. I heard Trisha scream, "Look out for the bridge." Traveling at the speed limit of 55 mph Marlin jerked the vehicle left to keep from hitting the bridge abutment. He overcompensated and almost hit the other side of the bridge. Never letting off the accelerator he narrowly missed hitting the bridge three more times. Finally he completely lost control and we tumbled down the hillside turning over 3 1/4 times. I never realized how a few seconds can seem so long. I thought we were never going to stop tumbling. The crushing of the vehicle overturning was quite disturbing. My thoughts immediately were: Are we going to make it to the airport today or are we going to get home safely at all. Finally we stopped tumbling, landing with the left side of the truck up. Everyone was asking if everyone else was OK. Marlin and Jennifer were able to get their doors open, and we all crawled out. Our suitcases had been thrown all over the ravine; one was torn open.

We started inspecting each other. I knew I was bleeding as I had warm blood running down my face from my forehead. Everyone else seemed to be O.K. except for a few bruises. After we seemed to check out OK, I asked everyone to join hands and I led us in prayer thanking God for safe delivery from the accident. We were grateful no one was seriously hurt. Marlin couldn't reach the group ahead of us on the cell phone, but was able to get someone in Olanchito, who in turn called and informed the group to come back for us. We then went on to the airport in La Ceiba. Pastor Dario kept saying, "I can't believe this happened. Are you sure you are O.K.?"

It was a fantastic week of adventure for the group. We all enjoyed it immensely. The people were so friendly and grateful for our services and our ministry. Most were very receptive to our evangelical efforts.

Most all the group, including me, would like to return one day. Next time I would like to trek up into the mountains. I estimate we saw approximately 1,100 people that week. Dario led several in the villages to accept Jesus as Savior. Using the Evangicube I led five to accept Jesus. I left three Evangicubes with different people to further witness about Jesus.

CHAPTER 26

The Amazon River

June 2004, July 2005

During the Baptist Medical Dental Fellowship meeting in 2002 I was attracted to a booth that was named Amazon Outreach. I took one of their brochures and was encouraged by the attendant at the booth to consider going on a large river boat down the Amazon River. He showed pictures of the boat and scenes along the Amazon River. That sounded intriguing, so I mentioned it to Dr. Dale Twilley, a dentist from Toccoa, Georgia. He seemed interested in this, so we talked about going the next year.

In April 2003, Dale called and asked me to go with a group from his church on an Amazon Outreach trip. I would have loved to have gone, but my daughter-in-law, son, and wife insisted I be present during the birth of our first grandson. I told them I would get back in plenty of time for the "event". But, they insisted I shouldn't be off in a foreign country at that time. Anyway, Dale and his group went and had a great trip.

In early 2004, Dale called again and wanted me to go on another trip to the Amazon River. I was eager and available to go this time. Dale had enlisted a relatively large group from First Baptist Church of Toccoa, Georgia, to go on the Amazon Outreach river boat.

According to its brochure, Amazon Outreach is a nondenominational, nonprofit mission organization formed to unite North and South Americans in spreading the Gospel message of Jesus Christ to the Amazon Basin in Brazil.

Friends of Dale from Louisiana, Tennessee, and North Carolina who had been on previous mission trips met with the Georgia group in the Miami Airport. We flew to Manaus, Brazil, arriving there at 3 a.m. We went straight to the Linda Esperanza, a three-decker river boat. It was the nicest I saw on the river all week. After traveling seventeen hours overnight we chose a hammock on the second or third deck and went to sleep. We awoke to a big delicious breakfast. Then we started down the river, traveling to our first destination for the next twenty-six hours except for a short nap for the captain.

The river was muddy and wide. Frequently it seemed to fill the entire horizon. Several houses on stilts and livestock could be seen just off the riverbank. The forest was quite thick in places, which is typical of a rainforest. Late that morning we started up a tributary which quickly narrowed to where it looked as if only a canoe could pass. The river boat just separated the aquatic growth and kept going. Soon we slowed, having to cut branches off trees on one side or the other to get the river boat past. At one point a hornet stung one of our Brazilian interpreters. We quickly applied ice and gave her Benadryl. Slowly and progressively our boat made it up the ever-narrowing tributary for over two hours to our destination, the village of Manaus. This was the first time a group of medical missionaries had visited this village. The people were very receptive. We held a medical-and-dental clinic for the remainder of the afternoon. We were just below the equator so the days and nights are almost evenly divided. It seemed to get dark rapidly. That night we had a worship service at the local school building where we had held the clinic that day. We sang with the people and listened to a short sermon by our Brazilian minister. Then in our boat we headed out from the shoreline approximately one-half mile to get away from the mosquitoes to spend the night. The nights were fairly cool, and a blanket was required before dawn.

After breakfast the next morning we went back into the village and worked until 2 p.m. when it seemed that everyone who wanted to be seen had been seen. I helped Dale extract teeth as the dental line always seemed longer than any other line, and we had essentially finished the medical clinic. The spiritual station was staffed by the Brazilian Presbyterian minister who frequently works with Amazon Outreach. He did most of the evangelizing. We then loaded back onto the Linda Esperanza and went back through the small tributary to the main river. We saw several pink dolphins making graceful appearances by rolling gently forward showing their dorsal fin. We noticed several more along the edge of the main river as we started down stream.

On June 2, we landed at Encinado. We made our way into the public school and held a medical-and-dental clinic. Meanwhile the Vacation Bible School and hair-cutting groups were busy working with the people.

Not long after the clinic started I was asked to go down river to see a sick man who couldn't travel to the clinic. We went in one of the "speed boats", an aluminum boat with an outboard motor, two miles down the river to a small house along the riverbank. There we found a middle-aged man complaining of lower abdominal pain. The exam revealed exquisite right-lower-quadrant tenderness in the abdomen very typical of acute appendicitis. I told him that he would have to go to the local hospital two hours away for surgery. I wasn't aware whether the boat had the material and resources to do that kind of surgery on the boat and knew we were leaving the area the next morning.

We had a good clinic. I once again helped Dale extract teeth as the dental-clinic line never seemed to shorten. Several people accepted Jesus as Savior during this and all the clinics.

On June 3 we arrived at Amadiou and set up clinic in the public-school area. I was asked to make a house call on an elderly lady near our boat-landing site. I found an 80-year lady who had pneumonia and had been vomiting, so I started an IV and gave her some IV fluid and IV antibiotics, and IV Phenergan. She was much better by the end of the day and was sitting outside on the front porch.

Later I was asked to go see another lady three miles down the river. On arrival there we had to go to the back of her home and knock loudly before she finally came to the door. Most of her nose had been eaten away by basal-cell carcinoma. I gave her some meds, then presented the Evangicube to her to make sure of her salvation. We had prayer with her. She was so grateful.

That night almost everyone took turns going out in the aluminum boats alligator hunting. The boat I was in had a few sightings, but we never got close enough to catch one. However, the other boat caught a 2-foot and a 5-foot alligator. The crew had thoroughly taped their mouths shut for safety sake in the boat.

On June 4 we pulled into Concaicao where no medical team had ever been before. We ministered to the people for a few hours while much of the time a tropical downpour occurred. Again several people accepted Jesus as Savior. We then packed up and started the long journey back to Manaus. We had a lot of fellowship on the 30-hour trip back. On the way we stopped at the "Stuckey's on the Amazon" souvenir shop and looked at a few alligators that were down a path to a pond in the tropical forest.

On June 6 we arrived back at Manaus, our site of origin. We went to the Tropical Hotel. Several went swimming, but a few like me crashed for a couple of hours. Then I went shopping in the small mall in the hotel complex and bought a few more souvenirs. I also looked at the Tropical Hotel Zoo.

That evening we went to Gaucho's restaurant, a *churrascaria*, and had all the meat we wanted to eat of many different varieties. We had good fellowship with the Brazilians one last time before we left for home.

The trip was a fantastic and rewarding. Jed Thomson, head of Amazon Outreach, had been on the boat initially for a short while before leaving on the next stop down river. He told our group he was planning a second mission boat and a safe-water-well boat for drilling for water in the villages, so the local people could have a safe-and-reliable source of water. He said while the wells are being drilled and instructions given for maintenance of the wells, opportunities will abound for the Gospel of Jesus Christ to be shared.

During the trip 839 medical patients and 164 dental patients were treated, 110 haircuts and 156 clothes distributions occurred, and 1,653 prescriptions were filled. Dale wrote me a thank-you note and gave me a report of all the statistics. He wrote that due to the excitement about the trip, he had already scheduled another trip down the Amazon the next July.

Dr. Dale Twilley asked me to be medical coordinator again in 2005. I ordered the meds and supplies and invited a friend, Jarrett Rule, a nurse practitioner who works at DeSoto Regional Health System in Mansfield, La. Dale had a large group from his church in Toccoa going again, but also had invited his reliable friends from Tennessee, Charles Manley and his sister, Nancy Mikkelson, with her husband, Mike.

Somehow Jarrett didn't get a proper visa picture to the Brazilian Embassy until five days before we left for Brazil. The Brazilian Embassy said the earliest we could get it was Friday, the day we were to leaving at 7 a.m. from Shreveport. I called Jarrett the night before and he told me he might not be going with us. I told him that everything would be OK and that I would see him at the airport at 6 a.m. the next morning.

At 6 a.m. I saw Jarrett at the Shreveport Regional Airport and told him he was indeed stepping out on faith. He wouldn't know if he could get his visa and passport until one hour before we left for Brazil. The visa was being sent from Houston to Miami by courier. The passport with the visa in it arrived 35 minutes before we boarded for Brazil. Yes, Jarrett got out of the boat and practically walked on water that day. Yes, prayer does work. Needless to say we were all relieved that he got it in time to board the plane with us or it would have been a long way back home with a broken heart.

Our big plane was broken, so we had to fly on a smaller plane and get it refueled in Panama City before we could fly on to Manaus, Brazil. We finally arrived in Manaus at 6 a.m., then went on to the boat at daybreak. We traveled on the Linda Esperanza, the same boat we were on the previous year. We had breakfast and headed down the Rio Negro River to where the Solomon River joins it and forms the giant Amazon River. The muddy waters of the Solomon stayed separated from the dark clear water of the Rio Negro for a few miles before they finally merge and become muddy much like the Solomon River.

We finally got to take a nap while going on down river to Parachins where we picked up Rev. Chad Sikes, an independent missionary to the Amazon River Basin. Many of us got to hear about his ministry on the Amazon River, beginning with his dreams to become a missionary and to a land he couldn't identify until he happened to visit a short time later with a good friend on a business trip. He subsequently went to seminary and later moved to Parachins. The Parachins Baptist Church, to which he now belongs, ministers to nearly 500 villages along the Amazon River and its many tributaries. Chad's organization is called Christ for the Amazon. He raises funds through this organization for his ministries. Then he told us how he works. He calls his program VIP for "visitation, implementation, and presentation". He explained how he believes the Catholic Church in Brazil is idolatrous, especially in its worship of Mary and many other statues. There is also much spiritualism, witchcraft, and sorcery. These people live in darkness; and are 500 years behind the Catholics in North America, he said.

The Visitation part is followed by the Implementation phase, which is so important for those who have initially accepted Jesus as Savior. They need and are presented Bible study. The Presentation phase is done by a trained pastor, but all three stages are going on at the same time.

Chad further related that the people are under a huge burden of sacrifice, especially to Mary. The Vatican and Catholics are the biggest land owners in Brazil, he said. Catholicism is forced on the people. When Protestants come in, people there who accept their methods are often rejected. Chad related that the people on the Amazon are humble and good people, but persecution is dominant, especially when it comes to monetary things. He says Catholics are bribed into following the church methods.

Chad said, "The Assembly of God has come to the Amazon, but they fail to followup because they bring no Bibles, no tracts, etc.

According to Chad the Christian villages are healthy and clean, but the non-Christian villages are dirty because they are without God. Some of Chad's statements may be inflammatory to some people, but they certainly make sense to me.

After listening to Chad and traveling 32 hours down the Amazon River and one of its tributaries, we arrived at Monte Carmelo. We were welcomed by a few villagers. One was the assistant pastor of the local church, who showed us the central assembly building which was being used for wood work. The pastor said he would have it cleaned out by the next morning for us to use as a clinic.

Marcos, the Brazilian representative of Amazon Outreach, mentioned going on down the river to the next village if we got through in time the next day. Chad conferred with Marcos, and they decided to invite the other village to come by boat to Monte Carmelo. I went by "speed boat" with Marcos, Chad, and the pastor from Monte Carmelo, and our driver to the village to invite them to the clinic. We arrived about 20 minutes before dark. The thick jungle seemed rather uninviting this time of day. The almost full moon helped with our vision. The people at the village were receptive to the idea of traveling to the clinic in Monte Carmelo the next day, but there was an issue, gasoline—so we siphoned four gallons of gasoline from our tank and gave it to them.

We were asked to make a house call in that village about one quarter of mile back up the river. We went to a grass hut which had only a small kerosene lamp lighting it. In a hammock lay an elderly man who appeared emaciated. An exchange in Portugese between the old man and Marcos revealed multiple problems. I was told he had been confined to that hammock for seven months and was too weak to walk. On exam the old man reeked of the smell of stale urine. He had complete cataracts, making him blind; he was frail and appeared tired. He had marked muscular wasting from the prolonged bed rest. I related to Marco that he was blind and debilitated to such an extent that I could do little for him.

Marcos and the old man proceeded to talk for over five more minutes. I was pleased that Marco presented the Gospel and the man accepted Jesus as Savior. That was all we could really do to help him.

The following morning we held medical-and-dental clinic at Monte Carmelo and also offered hair cutting, Vacation Bible School, and evangelism. Several from the village we had visited the previous night arrived by boat to be seen and treated. Several accepted Jesus as Savior.

We then proceeded to the next stop at Guarantuba where we spent the night on the river boat. The next morning we started clinic and held it until everyone was seen. Then we held a worship-and-celebration service. During the day Fah, my interpreter, and two of the river boat crew went with us to see an elderly man who was too ill with diarrhea and dehydration to make it to the clinic. I made Fah, a nursing student, a little nervous when I ran 2,000 cc of IV fluid with antibiotics in over 40 minutes, but the man did well, so we left him some oral meds to take over the next week. The people were very happy and appreciative.

On Wednesday, July 20, at Monte Gerezin we held our largest and longest clinic. Not long after we started boat loads of people wanting to be seen started arriving from across the river. Most of us were out under trees holding clinic. Jarrett and Nancy were seeing just as many patients as I did; they were hard workers. Once again, I made a house call just adjacent to the boat to see an ill man with nausea, vomiting, and diarrhea. I gave him IV fluids and Phenergan. He was asleep when we left. That evening about dark we held worship services in front of their church because the church was not large enough to hold all the people.

Stepping out of the shower that night wearing wet flip-flops, I slipped and landed hard on my left side and arm. I was sure I had broken some ribs. I envisioned having to have a chest tube. But amazingly I took two Aleve and wasn't bothered too much other than a bit of soreness. The next day a large hematoma showed up on my ventral left arm. Later when I got home I had my ribs x-rayed which showed five broken ribs. I learned first hand that it really does take 6 weeks for ribs to heal to the point there is no further pain.

The next day we went up the river to Boa Vista to hold clinic. We saw all that wanted to be seen. Five missionary interns lived in the village training to be full-time missionaries. According to Chad, part of their training was at the seminary. The interns were part of the Parachins group. We were invited to inspect their home and found it had running water, a shower, and many of the amenities of home.

We finished clinic early. Those who wanted were invited to hike into the forest to see where they were getting lumber to build their church. This adventure provided a first-hand look at a rainforest in the dry season. Three large trees had been cut down and boards were sawed by a chain saw in a near-perfect line. I asked them how they cut these so straight and was told it was done by "popping a line and sawing on the line". As you can imagine, the forest was thick with a lot of undergrowth. The shade of the trees did little to counter the tropical heat.

That night we had worship services inside the church. The main message was brought by one of the missionary interns.

Starting Thursday night and all-day Friday we journeyed

40 hours back to Manaus. I know this sounds strange, but we all almost tired of eating, but the food was so good.

We had seen over 700 people medically, dentally, and with our other services, but the best part was that 142 people accepted Jesus as Savior. The folks were so friendly on our team. It was a great trip.

Saturday morning we went shopping on the Amazon River for native crafts. While at the souvenir shop we got to see the new Amazon Outreach boat which was just like the one we had been on all week but better equipped. That night we went to Gaucho's Restaurant to eat and fellowship one more time with the Brazilian workers we had been with all week. Since a new team was not due that night, we spent one more night on the river boat before we left for the airport and returned to Miami. Some of us had to spend that night in Miami, as our flights could not resume until the next day.

CHAPTER 27

Cambodia

November 2004, November 2005

Surprised to get a phone call from Chris Sexton, I returned the call as soon as I could. Chris grew up in our church and was the son of some of our good friends. When I reached Chris in Dallas he said a good friend in his Sunday School Class at First Baptist Church in Carrollton, Texas, was an IMB missionary and headed back to Cambodia soon. He said the missionary needed some volunteers to do medical missions in Cambodia. He asked me to call Tony Pitaniello, the missionary.

Some friends of mine who had been on previous mission trips had related how wide open a mission field Cambodia had become. They told me if I ever got a chance to go to Cambodia I should leap at the opportunity.

After saying a brief prayer, I called Tony and was cordially greeted. We talked about his being in Dallas so Trish, his wife, could have their third child by C-section. He said they were anxious to get back to Cambodia after being stateside for almost a year. Tony then told me he needed eight medical-mission teams to visit his area of Kampong Cham over the next 12 months. He said he had made a deal with the Cambodian government guaranteeing the eight visits if they would allow him to do any at all. The more we talked, the more I was intrigued to go and serve with Tony and Trish. We discussed a timeframe that included my schedule, his schedule, and the weather patterns in Cambodia. (Having been in Vietnam I knew the regional monsoon weather pattern.) Tony already had scheduled one group to arrive in late September/early October. We agreed that early November would be an ideal time for both of us. I was quite excited about the opportunity to serve with IMB missionaries in Cambodia.

I immediately started recruiting volunteers for the trip. I put out an email to all my mission buddies. I called the Baptist Medical Dental Fellowship organization in Memphis and asked it to put out a request for volunteers for a trip to Cambodia November 8-18, 2004. I called some of my local friends such as Rev. and Mrs. Sonny DePrang, who after praying about it decided to go. After I persuaded Jackie to go, she encouraged my wife, Vickie, to go. Don Salyer, a registered pharmacist from Mabank, Texas, also agreed to go. I began to tell all my acquaintances at work that I needed help on a trip to Cambodia. Dr. Fred Sullivan and Fran Norsworthy, R.N., of the Natchitoches area, volunteered to go also.

Following Tony's advice I got tickets for us through MTS Travel Agency. Heather Calabove at the agency was most helpful. Then I ordered meds, supplies, and arranged to get traveling, health, and evacuation insurance for us.

The airplane flight to Phnom Penh through Dallas, Los Angeles, Taipei and on to Cambodia was long. Tony was waiting for us at the airport. I readily recognized him from his picture that he had sent us by email. We had no problems getting six trunks of meds and supplies through customs as I had emailed Tony a list of meds with names, quantity, lot number, and expiration date a month earlier. He obtained a certified list with approval from the Minister of Health earlier (actually the day before). We literally just walked through customs.

We were weary, but Tony wanted us to visit his home first and see his son who had been sick all day with a fever of 104. It just happened that Dr. Sullivan was a board-certified pediatrician (in addition to being an emergency-room physician). After meeting Trish and the family, Fred treated Joshua for a middle-ear infection. The Pitaniellos home was quite nice, but had no air conditioning.

Tony then took us downtown to the Hawaii Hotel for the night and for some much-needed sleep. The next morning we drove to Kampong Cham, about sixty miles northeast of Phnom Penh. The countryside was lush and green in several places. We saw many rice fields, but most were empty as it was the dry season in Cambodia. We stopped along the way and picked up Abuss, a pastor/interpreter who would work with us for the week. The pastor was Tony's first convert, and he was still working with Tony. We noted several clay-brick factories along the highway. The road was asphalt and in good condition. Tony told us that the Cambodian president was from Kampong Cham which made a good road from Phnom Penh to Kampong Cham a high priority.

After dropping off our suitcases at the Mekong River Hotel, where we would spend the next five days, we headed for Tool Balay, approximately twelve miles further off the main road. This was a village of 1,000 into which Tony had brought previous groups to work. Tony had good rapport with the Islam chief who even let Tony make announcements and preach the Gospel on the loud speaker there. We were readily greeted by the villagers and almost immediately started clinic. By the time we left the first evening, we had seen forty-one patients. The following three days we held all-day clinics.

Dr. Fred and I did a couple of minor surgeries, and I

extracted about sixty necrotic teeth. It was obvious that no dental care was at hand there.

By the end of the second day, it was quite hot in the small house in which we were working; no air was circulating. I told Tony we had to have fans. Being the congenial fellow he is, Tony had a small generator and four fans the next morning before we started to work. These turned out to be life savers. We left our meds at the small house where we were working because people there were so trustworthy.

The people also were very friendly and appreciative. Most impressive was the spiritual response. Jackie and Tony triaged the patients. Fred and I treated the patients. Don and Vickie worked in the pharmacy. The Holy Spirit was in charge in the spiritual station! Tony and other groups worked with the people, and the field was white for the harvest. Of the 376 sent to the spiritual station, 315 in Tool Balay accepted Jesus as Savior. The last day we had more people accept Jesus than we had as patients. Teenagers and older kids came up the back step to the spiritual station and after listening to the Gospel presentation using the Evangicube, accepted Jesus also. Words cannot magnify the phenomenal event. That, my friend, is what medical missions is all about: evangelism. Rev. Sonny DePrang was so excited about the results while he and the pastor/interpreter worked at the spiritual station, that he wanted to return in 2005. In fact, my whole team plus many more returned later.

Tony had told us that by holding a clinic we could reach more people in one week than he could reach using other methods in a year. He is the most compassionate missionary with whom we have ever worked in terms of getting the job done.

The fifth working day we went to a village just outside the

city limits of Kampong Cham. We saw twenty-five more people and made one house call on an elderly gentleman who couldn't walk. Sonny did a short presentation of the Gospel and three more accepted Jesus as Savior, but most left immediately after getting their meds. They missed the real reason we were there.

We had 318 professions of faith in Jesus in three whole days and two half days of clinic. The acceptance rate was over 80%. The Lord really used Sonny to lead all these folks to Jesus! Tony said he would follow up with these people shortly with an evangelical team that was scheduled to arrive soon. Tony hopes to get the people to start a church in Tool Balay.

On the way back to Phnom Penh Tony offered to stop for anyone who wanted some fried tarantulas. Surprisingly, he had no takers. Shortly after arriving at the Pitaniello's home we ate pizza. The children had been sick all week, and Trish was unable to join our group in Kampong Cham.

The next morning Tony and Trish took us to the market place where we bought a lot of souvenirs because they were relatively inexpensive. We ate lunch at a restaurant where a Christian woman hires young women who are former prostitutes trying to get back to a normal life.

Then we went to one of the genocide museums: Tuol Sleng. Seeing part of the "Killing Fields" was so sad, but it served us a reminder of what should never happen again. There were pictures of many people who had been tortured and killed there, as well as many skulls and other relics to show some of the horrendous acts that had been done. To give you an idea of the magnitude of the Killing Fields, neighboring Vietnam now has 77 million people, Thailand has 66 million people; but Cambodia has only 13 million people now, according to Tony.

We drove by the King of Cambodia's palace, then downtown to the mall, which is very modern.

We had a fantastic trip, one that is difficult to describe in words when you look at the spiritual results. All my group committed to return in November 2005. Tony challenged us to bring a large enough group to minister to a western Cham village of 10,000, an Islamic stronghold never exposed to the love of Jesus.

By October 2005 I had gathered 19 to return to Cambodia to serve with the Pitaniello's. These folks were from five states. I took my wife, church friends, people who I had met on previous medical mission trips, people I got to know from the internet through the Baptist Medical Dental Fellowship, and friends of my missions friends. The Lord certainly had a hand in formation of this group of the best folks with whom I have ever served. I will always cherish those that volunteered to go on this trip.

Tony told me ahead of time that the village of 10,000 would have to be later because the road had just been washed out and we did not have a safe haven to stay at night. We agreed to return to the same area as 2004.

On November 7, 2005, we went by different routes and times to meet all on the same day in Phnom Penh. Included in our group was Dr. Rama, a native Cambodian who escaped the "killing fields" in 1979 at the age of 11. Tony arranged to pick up all of us at the airport. We went to his home to have lunch with Trish and the family. My, how his children had grown since last November.

The following morning we traveled via vans to Kampong Cham, left our suitcases in the Mekong Hotel on the Mekong River, and after a brief lunch went straight to the village of Gong Go about twelve miles away, and set up clinic and started working. We had five doctors, six nurses, four ministers, and enough members to form three teams. Every one graciously followed my suggestion about which team to be assigned. Tony had rented three homes that were all close to each other for us to hold the clinics. I was the "dentist" and mostly extracted teeth all week. We worked three hours the first day.

The people were very grateful. They came by the hundreds. Gong Go is a village of 3,000 Western Cham people. It is just down the road from where our team had worked the previous year. Our three groups saw 1,136 patients over five working days. Fred Sullivan, M.D., did a couple of minor surgeries. I extracted 350 necrotic teeth. Most of the things we saw were common maladies, such as pain from working all day every day. Then there were some of the unusual things also, as well as some surgical problems we could not handle in the field.

Of these patients 801 accepted Jesus as Savior. Tony had the ministers serving in the spiritual station use a chart he and a group had worked on for months to present the Gospel. This chart ("towel" as Tony called it) showed the history of God creating Adam and Eve, Adam and Eve eating the forbidden fruit, Noah and the Ark, Abraham going up to sacrifice Isaac, Moses leading the Israelites out of Egypt, Jesus (Isa) being born in a stable, Jesus raising Lazarus from the dead, Jesus dying on the cross to pay for our sins, Jesus after three days returning to life; and finally Jesus ascending into Heaven. This tied in with their Muslim knowledge of Abraham and Moses and presented Jesus as the Redeemer of the world. Tony's chart worked out well; it was accepted by a large proportion of the people.

At lunch time Rev. Robert Finley and some of the others went out in the streets and village to presented the Gospel using the Evangicube. Some 200 more accepted Jesus as Savior. It was a great spiritual week. The group instantly bonded and worked well together.

One night after supper at our one main restaurant in Kampong Cham at my request Dr. Rama told his story of his family surviving the "killing fields". Dr. Rama's dad went to one of the communist meetings one night and never returned home. Dr. Rama told of his personal experience where he first was enticed to join the communists and spy on his friends. Due to injuries this did not pan out. Later he escaped while being fired at with rifles. He made it to the Thailand border where he was later evacuated. Most of his family survived. He wanted to return to Cambodia for the first time since leaving Cambodia to visit his remaining relatives. My, what a touching saga he gave. By the end of his story not a dry eye was in the room.

On Nov. 17 we returned to Phnom Penh and ate supper at the Pitaniello's home. The following day we went shopping at one of the local native shops. I thought women were the best shoppers, but Kevin Andrews and Ron Townsend could out-bargain the best. After lunch some went to the Tuol Slang (SR-21 School) or "Killing Fields Museum" in town. They will remember that forever. The museum presents the gruesome facts of what happened in and around Cambodia between 1975 and 1979.

The next night we ate supper at the poolside of the Billagong Hotel while fireworks went off in the night celebrating the Water Festival. Masses of people turned out during the week in Phnom Penh for that celebration.

The following day we all went to the airport to return the long way home. Tony and Trish were such great hostesses. They truly have a passion, compassion, and love for the people of Cambodia. This is so evident in the work they have done, are doing, and plan to do. We got to serve as ambassadors for Jesus Christ with some great IMB missionaries.

Tony and I had already made plans for the trip next year to a larger village down the main road east where 3,500 Cham people await to hear the good news of the Gospel.

Within a few months I had 30 people signed up to go back to Cambodia in 2006. About that time Tony emailed me and gave me the good news and the bad news:

— The good news: Tony and Trish are expecting their fourth child. The baby is to be born by repeat C-section, requiring a trip to Bangkok, Thailand.

— The bad news: The baby is due the day we were scheduled to arrive in Cambodia. This means that we will have to wait until November 2007 to return to serve once again with the Pitaniello's.

Chapter 28

Return to North Benin

January 2005

Finally Suzanne and John Crocker were back in Kare, Togo, and ministering to the Ditarmari people in north Togo and Benin. T.I.M.E. (Training in Ministerial Evangelism) Ministries was going to north Benin again to serve with the Crockers—like we did in November 2002 when Dr. Larry Daniels and I had gone with a small medical team to minister to the people in Natitingou and some surrounding villages.

I was asked to gather a medical team and to go ahead of the evangelical team so we could clear the meds through the Minister of Health, go north from Cotonou to Natitingou, and start our medical clinic in the new Natitingou Baptist Church.

Dr. Larry Daniels was asked to go with us again and said he would, but apparently he got lost somewhere along the way. Another doctor from Georgia was going with us, but her husband became ill and she had to drop out. Finally, Dr. Ron Collins, who was engaged to John Crocker's sister, volunteered to go with us. Also his sister, Diane, a x-ray technician, volunteered to go with us.

Trent Wallace, a pharmacist from Tennessee, who had been on trips with me to Brazil, had asked me to let him know if I were ever going to Africa again; I emailed him, and indeed he did want to go with us.

Ron Townsend, fireman, and his wife, Amy, R.N., had served with the Crockers the previous year and wanted to go back, so they were added to the team.

Then a good friend of mine, Rev. Stan Horton, who had recently been ordained as a minister of intercessory prayer, was invited. Hospital administrators where he worked as chaplain had told him that if he ever wanted to go on a volunteer foreign mission trip, they would fund his way. I told him of the success with the Evangicube, and he obtained one with which to practice and learn the technique. He was excited about going.

So, our team was set. Beverly Wisdom, secretary to Dr. Thomassian (T.I.M.E. Ministries director), proceeded to get our airplane tickets.

Our team met in the Atlanta Airport where new acquaintances were made; then we flew via Air France through Paris to Cotonou.

When we arrived in Cotonou, we were greeted by Judy Miller, John Crocker, and Lin Pinter, all IMB missionaries to Benin/Togo area. We spent the night at the Baptist Mission House. It was pleasantly cool for a change. The next morning we found out why: the *harmattan*, the annual Sahara dust storm, was nearly blotting out the sun. Visibility was less than one-half mile. We went to get our meds approved at the Minister of Health's office, but he was not available until after 2 p.m. Judy told him we could not wait until then and still make it to Natitingou by dark (about 6 p.m.), since it was at least an eight-hour drive. The Minister of Health then said to bring two of the six trunks to his office to be inspected. Judy agreed. The evangelical team could bring them north in two days.

Cyprien, my interpreter from my trips to south Benin in

2000 and 2001, had volunteered to go with us. I had kept in contact with him through the years by email. When I told him we were going to Natitingou, he wanted to go with us as an interpreter. I also got to see him baptized in 2001. As requested he met us at the chosen hour at the Baptist Mission House ready to travel north with us.

Our caravan of three vehicles took off north toward Natitingou. Along the way Judy was considerate to stop a few times for some great photo ops ("Kodak moments"). I got a good photo of a real recent voodoo shrine along the highway. National Voodoo Day was the previous day. When I got out and took a photo, the locals started screaming at us, so we took flight and were quickly on our way north again. Next we stopped to look and take photos of two huge vipers (the snakes we saw were three- to four-feet long), which were on sale for human consumption. Further along the way, we stopped to look and take photos of a big bush rat (the body was at least 15 inches long), and rabbits stretched and heat dried—all ready for someone to enjoy for lunch.

About halfway to Natitingou we stopped at Judy Miller's friends, a married couple who are IMB missionaries to Benin. He was interpreting and writing a local dialect for the Old and New Testament. They were literally in the middle of nowhere and glad to have us for a brief visit. Ron let the missionary wife call her mother on his satellite phone. She was thrilled to talk with her mother as if she were right next door.

We arrived at the Tata Somba Hotel shortly before dark. This was where we had stayed in November 2000 when we worked previously with John and Suzanne.

We started work the next morning in the new Baptist church for which T.I.M.E. Ministries had donated the costs for materials and construction. One of our first patients was the donor of the land on which the new church was built. The site was little more than a literal dump until used for the new church. We were soon enveloped with more people than we could really treat. We saw patients from infants to adults in their seventies. We treated, gave meds, extracted teeth; then sent them to the pharmacy for "free" meds. Then it was on to the most important station: the spiritual station. Rev. Stan Horton and IMB missionary Lin Pinter, along with Cyprien work there. Occasionally they would need a third-party interpreter, usually for the Datamari language, to get the message across. They started off with two or three people at a time. When we got busy, they had eight, ten, or twelve people at one time showing and telling them the Gospel using the Evangicube.

Phoebe, the Assembly of God minister who runs an orphanage on the outskirts of the city, brought eight small babies to our clinic. Phoebe will take any baby while another orphanage nearby refuses any sick or dirty baby. Two were quite ill—one more so than the other—from diarrhea, vomiting, and dehydration. The sickest baby was a recent admit to her orphanage and required hospitalization for a week. The infant still had a heparin lock in her wrist where Phoebe was giving IV antibiotics at the orphanage. We gave IM antibiotics to both and asked Phoebe to bring the babies back to our clinic the next day. The heparin lock was removed as it was not functional.

By the end of the first day, we began having a little problem with crowd control. That got worse the second day, especially when time began to run out. Even the pastor had difficulty controlling the crowd.

Phoebe brought the two babies back as requested. One was definitely better, but the child that had been hospitalized and sent home with a heparin lock, looked worse. We sent for IV fluids and gave IV antibiotics and fluid. Within three hours the baby was even worse. We told Phoebe the baby was going to die. There was not a dry eye in the clinic. The baby died three hours later after Phoebe took her back to the orphanage.

All the evangelical team came by motor vehicle. Dr. Thomassian was to fly north via private plane, but due to the *harmattan*, he too had to drive. They came into Natitingou and immediately started going to schools, prisons, churches, and the market to evangelize with their puppets, dramas, and evangelical preaching.

Meanwhile, we moved our team to Boukombe, the capital city of the Ditamari people. Natitingou is the frontier and business capital of the Ditamari people. Boukombe was the place where we lost crowd control at the health center in 2002. When we arrived there Suzanne got in touch with the village chief and went searching for a more ideal place. While they were looking, we prayerwalked around the health center.

In about 30 minutes, Suzanne returned with great news. She had located a house with a seven-foot concrete wall surrounding it one-half mile up the road. It was an ideal place for crowd control. Dr. Ron, Suzanne, Amy, Ron, Diane and I then saw approximately 1,300 people over the next three days. We treated such things as malaria, scabies, multiple skin disorders, pain of every description, and eye disorders, especially eye irritation associated with the *harmattan*. I extracted about 125 teeth during the week.

Saturday Dr. Thomassian and the evangelical team formally dedicated the Natitingou Baptist Church. We all went to church there on Sunday. We enjoyed the puppets, dramas, and sermon by Dr. Thomassian. John Crocker translated the sermon in French.

That afternoon several of the medical team went out to the orphanage at Phoebe's request to do some circumcisions. The first young boy was about five years old. Once I got started, he kept saying the same statement over, and over, and over. Finally I asked my interpreter what he was saying. The interpreter said, "He is saying: Oh white man; Oh white man; Oh white man." Actually I used a penile block and after this was given, the surgery was painless. Operating on the kitchen table, I was able to do ten circumcisions before light faded from the sunlight coming through the window and my flashlight batteries failed.

Suzanne had told me that the orphanage had no safe source of water. A water drilling company had told them it would charge $8,000 to dig a deep well, but because it was an orphanage, they would do it for $800. Knowing this beforehand, our medical group collected $1,100 which we presented to Phoebe before we left. Gratification and joy took on a new meaning when our team presented this to her. Tears of joy were abundant. Phoebe let us know that the work we had done for them was more than she could earn in over 100 days of work.

We finished up the Boukombe clinic the next day. As a team we saw 2,150 people in five working days (this included the orphanage on Sunday). Of that number 744 accepted Jesus as Lord and Savior. We were all amazed at the results, but John and Suzanne had been laying the ground work for this for years. The harvest was truly ready and the Holy Spirit did the rest. To God be the Glory!

Now John could proceed to form a church there soon. Stan took down the name and tribe of each individual who accepted Jesus, so they could be reached for followup. This means a church is going to be built right in the heart of Satan's nest.

Can you imagine what this may do for this city?

Cyprien was instrumental in the spiritual station. Stan allowed him to give the Evangicube presentations the last day. Due to the large crowds as many as twenty-five people were being seen at a time in the spiritual station. We are hoping Cyprien will continue doing this type of work. We left him an Evangicube.

As a team we had jelled quickly; we worked with a sweet team spirit that will not be soon forgotten. Amy and Ron Townsend want to be missionaries one day. I have not found any nicer with whom to work.

On our way back from Natitingou to Cotonou for our return flight home, we had a near tragic event. About five miles above Allada (35 miles from Cotonou) an accident occurred. We were traveling in a convoy of three vehicles, when the lead vehicle had to stop suddenly because of a large truck tanker. The second vehicle crashed into the back of the first, spilling luggage, clothes, and a bag containing our passports and money onto the street. When we reached the scene moments later, we were stricken with panic, fearing that one of our vehicles had struck and killed someone. Suddenly we were confronted by a hostile crowd of 100 to 200 people shouting, jeering and beginning to surround us. We were afraid of bodily harm from the people. As no police were available, we knew we were on our own. The people knew we were stranded, had money, and luggage. Trent and I searched quickly for a body, but found none. Cyprien had grown up in Allada and knew the language and people. He quickly defused a potential disaster. We escaped with all of our belongings. A wrecker was dispatched from Cotonou for the truck which had hit the SUV from behind rupturing the radiator. Stan led us in prayer. We were so thankful and grateful to escape unharmed. Although a bit crowded we made it to Cotonou in the two remaining vehicles.

John had worked with the evangelical team while Suzanne had worked with the medical team. They had worked to prepare for all the clinics and evangelism we had accomplished. It was so nice to have dedicated IMB missionaries on our team.

Words are not adequate for the accomplishments God allowed us to do and for all the gratitude we owe to those who worked with us.

CHAPTER 29

The Philippines

2005, 2006

In June 2004, Bro. Chad Grayson and his wife, Lenora, were staying at our home in Bossier City so they could start searching for a new house. Chad had been called almost unanimously to be our new pastor. I was a member of the pastor-search committee. The search had been a long struggle of two years to find the man we all wanted. I had emailed Chad and Lenora and invited them to stay at our home if they would like while searching for a home.

While staying with us, we got to talking about my favorite subject, missions. Chad said, "I have a good friend who is a missionary-pastor in Pampanga, the Philippines, an area northeast of Manila. Why don't you email him and tell him we are interested in bringing a medical-and-evangelical team to serve with him." I immediately emailed Rev. Alan Guevarra.

One week later I received a return email from Alan stating, "I would love for you to come." When I got that email I discussed with Chad what would be a good time for him to go. By then I had emailed Alan and he said, "Any time would be good for me." Chad looked at his calender and found that his best time to take off from seminary was the last week of February and early March. We chose to leave on a Monday so Chad would miss only one Sunday at church.

Then I got in touch with MTS Travel Agency which I had successfully used to go to Cambodia. Tickets were later ordered through them.

Recruitment for the trip went fairly smoothly. I sent out an email to people who had gone on trips with me previously. Buddy and Rose Mary Andrews and later Cullen and Joyce Keith joined the group wanting to go. While I was working in the ER at Natchitoches, La. I asked several to go on the trip with us. Dr. Fred Sullivan and Fran Norsworthy, R.N. wanted to go also. Don Salyer, pharmacist from Mabank, Texas, answered my email and volunteered to go. As departure time approached, I ordered medicines and medical and dental supplies.

Our flight took us through Memphis, Detroit, Nagoya (Japan), then on to Manila where Alan and Rolly, missionary pastors, were waiting to take us through customs, and then on to our hotel in San Fernando, Pampanga. We finally got to bed at 3 a.m., but we had to get up at 6 a.m. to get ready for the first day of clinic.

On February 23, we went to Sama, Baatan (mission outreach) to Pastor Rolly's church. We started clinic out under the mango trees and thatch straw buildings that were available. The spiritual station was in a thatch hut that the workers used for siestas during the work day. The pharmacy as well as the eye clinic were located in the shed of a thatch building. Fran and I were out under mango trees. It was obvious that it was meant for me to be a dentist that day (and the week), as I started seeing a large number of people with necrotic teeth. Joyce joined Fran later to handle the medical line as nurse practitioners. I was their consultant on any questions about any of the patients. Rose Mary and Buddy gave out reading glasses. Don and Vickie worked in the pharmacy. Chad and Cullen worked in the spiritual station effectively using the Evangicube. We saw 241 people that day and led 143 to faith in Christ. Chad was so excited. He had never used the Evangicube before, but he was a firm believer now that the Evangicube works. The weather was pretty warm in the afternoon, but pleasant in the shade. It was the dry season in the Philippines.

On February 24, we went to Wenceslao village, Lubao (mission outreach) and worked in the local school yard; we saw 334 patients and had 145 experience salvation. I was pulling more and more necrotic teeth. That night we went to a revival at the Good News Baptist Church (Rev. Rico's church) where Chad gave an inspiring and encouraging message to the members and a few guests. Rev Rico and his son sang a special song while playing their guitars. They did a fantastic job.

On February 25, we went to Pio Porac (mission outreach) where we saw 386 patients, out of which 198 accepted Jesus as Savior, and filled 1,386 prescriptions. I pulled almost 200 necrotic teeth, pulling 1 to 7 teeth per person. Alan told me the people couldn't afford dental care in town, and when they did go the dentists in town used little or no anesthesia. As the word spread, I had plenty of customers. We gave away 95 pair of reading glasses. This was the busiest day, out in the "cool 90 degrees" weather under mango trees.

Toward the end of the day, Chad came from the pharmacy and told me, "We are running out of vitamins, worm meds, and bandages." I told him, "We may be running out of medicines and bandages, but "You'll never run out of Jesus."

That night we went to a revival service at Calantas Baptist Church (Rev. Rolly Betero's church). Again Chad gave an encouraging and inspiring message.

On February 26, we went to Alan's church (Faith Baptist Mission Church) where he and Rolly also live in the building.

Alan had taken us to the property his church had bought on the main highway. He said they hoped to start construction of the church in the next couple of months. His lease on his church/house would be up in 3 months, and he would have to move out then. That day at his church, we saw 264 patients and 91 accepted Jesus as Savior.

On Sunday, February 27, we went back to Faith Baptist Mission Church for revival services. Cullen gave a short sermon, Joyce and I gave short testimonies, and Chad gave an encouragement-and-salvation sermon. For lunch, Alan finally took us to eat Filipino food at the mall. It was delicious. I ate at least half a dozen vegetables and several fruits I have never previously eaten; they were very good. After peanut-butter-and-jelly sandwiches at lunch every day, we at my insistence always came to the mall to eat supper. I did not want anyone getting ill from eating the wrong food. And, we didn't get sick the whole week because we had food from all the American places such as Burger King, McDonald's, Kentucky Fried Chicken, Pizza Hut, etc. The four-block-long mall had plenty of places from which to chose.

Sunday night we returned to Faith Baptist Missionary Church for another message from Chad. Cullen gave 45 large Gideon Bibles (King James Version in English) to the pastors of all the surrounding churches who had been invited to the service that night. Fran gave 60 Bibles (KJV in English) to the pastor's wives and members of Alan's congregation. Then each of our team was given a beautiful carved wooden name plague for our desks.

On February 28, as we were on our way to our next village, we saw pile after pile of volcano ash, some up to 30-feet high or more where a nearby volcano had erupted a few years ago, not far from Clark Air Force Base. The ash had covered everything for miles around and had killed many people.

Clark Air Force Base was abandoned by the Air Force because of the extensive damage. Not much further we came to the Haduan Tribal Mission Church. The village was actually on the edge of the mountains. We set up clinic on a ridge where for miles one could see the beautiful foliage and mountain ranges. The weather was much cooler in the mountains, and a gently refreshing breeze often came by. We finished up the 126 patients with 61 salvations by 2 p.m. The pastor from Burog Mission Church, about three miles further down the road, asked us to come to his church if possible. We had time, so we took the opportunity to minister at his church. Several members of our group turned down the opportunity to walk one mile and go across a foot bridge to a remote village. We would have had to carry in our supplies by foot.

We proceeded to the Burog Mission Church and saw 92 people with 70 salvations. The people there were the poorest and choose to live in the mountains and rarely ventured into town.

Alan's wife, Elnora, kept records for us all week. We saw a total of 1,443 people, and led 708 to accept Jesus as Savior. To God be the glory! Chad, Cullen, and our group were ecstatic about the results. We were so appreciative of the pastors and their families for all the work and support they gave us.

On March 1, we went via boat to Corrigador Island for an inspiring and educational adventure. There was a tremendous amount of history there—for instance, the site where General MacArthur was told to leave the island and left for Australia. He had said, "I will return." There are a wealth of historic relics there and the beautiful Pacific War Memorial. We thoroughly enjoyed the day.

On March 2, we were on our way to Mt. Sumat and Subic

Bay when one of the vans overheated and actually caught on fire; we had to put it out with water. We abandoned the field trip, but to make the best of the situation, we went souvenir shopping behind our hotel in a small market.

That night we all went to bed early as we had to rise the next morning at 2:30 a.m. to make it back to Manila in time to catch our return flight to the U.S. It was a great trip.

Alan and Rolly suggested donations to their churches so they could soon start construction on their buildings. Rolly stated, "I am going to name my church the Airline Baptist Mission Church of the Philippines." Plans were made for another trip to work with Alan, Rolly, and Rico the next year about the same time to dedicate their churches.

Through the providence of God I was able to recruit a team of eleven to return to Pampanga, the Philippines, in late 2005. We had seven different churches from Louisiana, Texas, Arkansas, and Tennessee represented in our new team. Bro. Chad Grayson was tied up with seminary, seminars, and church activities and couldn't go, so I practically volunteered for Bro. Harrell Shelton to go. Actually he was delighted to go on our mission trip. Rev. Harrell Shelton is the associate pastor of Airline Baptist Church and was instrumental in coordinating the building of our new facility that was built in 1995.

One of our ladies in the church, Barbara Pace, wanted her brother, Rev. Scotty Teague, to go on a mission trip with our church. I was given his home phone number and I called him in New York City where he has been a street evangelist for 25 years. He had been thinking about retiring and was in the process of leaving New York just before our trip started. He was delighted to go with us. Scotty is really reflective of the term "street evangelist". He has been faithful in all types of weather and through all types of harassment from the police,

Muslims, atheists, and other distractions in New York City to gladly present the Word of God to whoever would listen. He has used sketch drawings, puppets, and many other techniques to get the attention of the crowds in order to lead them to faith in our Lord Jesus Christ. His monthly or quarterly newsletter is always filled with stories of situations he has had to endure in order to share his faith with others.

The night before we left for the Philippines an ice storm developed in the southeast. All four bridges from Bossier City to Shreveport were frozen over. We had to delay our flights for one day. I was on the phone for hours rescheduling all our flights as we were flying from four different airports. Finally we all met in Detroit; then we flew to Manila after waiting in airports and flying for twenty-nine hours.

Missionary pastors Alan and Rolly met us at the airport. Alan once again had done all the legwork necessary to get approval through the local, district, regional and national levels for our mission trip. From the lists that I had emailed him, he got approval through the Minister of Health for our meds. We practically marched through the airport and speedily loaded in our vans to get to our hotel, which was a three-hour drive northeast to the city of San Fernando in the Pampanga district.

Alan and Rolly had coordinated with different pastors and churches to set up the clinics. The message was passed that we were coming and we expected larger crowds than we had the previous year. This year we had with us another physician, Dr. Bud Young, from Murfreesboro, Tennessee, whom I had met a few years earlier on a mission trip to Paraguay. Also Justina Rivera, R.N. from Antioch, Tennessee, came to run our eye clinic; she had ordered 5,000 pairs of eyeglasses from the Lion's Club in Virginia. She also had a few hundred reading glasses for those that needed them.

Clara Veatch, R.N. from Bossier City, was my nurse practitioner. She helped Dr. Bud with the medical patients. I was the dentist once again. Her husband, Wayne, helped Justina and Bryan Adams, a student from the Dallas, Texas, area in the eye clinic. The pharmacy was to be run by Don Salyer, R.PH., and Kaye Carter, R.N., from Bossier City. Glen Carter, R.N., started out as a nurse practitioner, but found it essential to help me in the dental clinic because I was so busy. Scotty and Harrell headed up our spiritual station where they used the teaching size (11" x 11") Evangicube to present the Gospel and salvation plan through Jesus Christ.

On Thursday, Feb. 23, we went to San Simon and worked at Pastor Catalan's church. Many people were evaluated and treated; and many accepted Jesus. I had started out by the church in the yard extracting teeth and was getting tired, hot, and frustrated by the workload. Glen saw my plight and came and helped me the remainder of the day and was my faithful and most helpful assistant for the other clinics.

The next day we went to Haduan, past Clark Air Force Base up in the edge of the mountains, to minister to the people. It was beautiful there with a cool mountain breeze most of the time. The second half of that day we went to the Light House Baptist Church in Sindalan where we were greeted with a very nice Filipino-prepared luncheon. We had a very busy clinic the remainder of the afternoon.

On Feb. 25 we went to Samal Bataan where Pastor Rolly has a missionary church out in the countryside. He has named the church there the Airline Baptist Mission of the Philippines. He pointed out his need for funds to put a new roof on the church and enlarge the building for a growing church membership.

The next day was Sunday and we went to Alan's new church on the main Bataan Highway; the year before it was just the empty lot he had shown us. With the help of funds from us and other sources, he was building a nice-sized church to minister to a fairly populated area in the district. We were delighted to listen to Dr. Bud Young's bass voice in a solo and later to Alan's sisters, Gemna and Bernadette. Alan gave his testimony and Scotty gave an awesome message. After lunch at the church we saw church members and church family for a few hours.

That Sunday night we went to a couple's "Love Banquet" where Dr. Bud sang and gave a talk on women. Scotty gave a wonderful sermon on marriage and love; mainly sex is not love, and love is not sex. Then we had some more good Filipino cooking.

On Feb. 27 we went to San Nicolas Lubao Church in Santa Rita to hold clinic. On Feb. 28 we went to Santa Catalina for the last clinic. The work was intense as we worked diligently seeing 1,160 in the medical clinic, 175 in the dental clinic with 304 teeth extracted. We filled almost 5,000 prescription and gave away 590 pairs of reading glasses.

But most important of all, Scotty and Harrell led 1,071 to accept Jesus as Savior. This further goes to prove what prayer can accomplish. We had our churches at home, staff at the International Mission Board, my Gideon camp, our families, and many others praying for us in our work and evangelical efforts. What an experience! God does work in a miraculous way with his people.

By the end of our trip we were all bone-tired. Nevertheless, we got up at 3 a.m. and went—despite the "state of emergency" with the recent bloodless coup in Manila—to Manila and went out to Corregidor on a tour boat seventeen miles out into the bay. The island is so full of history, especially about WWII. We took in all the history and sites for our R&R. It was marvelous.

We went back to our hotel early as he had to get up and leave at 1:30 a.m. to be at the airport in Manila in time for our flight back home.

Words are inadequate to express appreciation to my team members for their diligent work, the missionary pastors and local pastors who worked with us, the people themselves who were so gracious and appreciative, and all those at home who supported our efforts and prayed for us.

Our church plans a return trip back to the Philippines in 2007. As I told Alan and Rolly, "We shall return." Bro. Chad (Rev. Chad Grayson) has been invited back with the group in 2007 to formally dedicate the Airline Baptist Mission Church of the Philippines. Our mission group will also help dedicate Alan's church as our church because Jeff Lowe of Bossier City donated thousands of dollars to help finance the finishing of that church.

Chapter 30

"Intense and Unrelenting" Ghana

April 2006

I was invited by friends, Dr. Doug Parkin and his wife, Alice, to go to Ghana to work in the Baptist Medical Centre. Doug and I were interns together at Confederate Memorial Medical Center. I had not heard from them in years until I received an email from them telling about a real need for a surgeon at the hospital in Nalerigu. Doug and Alice were going to Ghana once or twice yearly to work at the hospital. I agreed to go in August 2005, but later had to postpone that because my wife, son, and daughter-in-law insisted I be present for the birth of my son and daughter-in-law's twins that would be due about the time I would be gone.

In November the Baptist Medical Dental Fellowship sent out an urgent email stating that physician-and-surgeon help was desperately needed at the Baptist Medical Centre in Nalerigu. I got in contact with the Parkins again and found out that Doug had had a heart attack and would not be able to go to Ghana for at least another year. I had been in touch with Dr. Bud Young about going to the Philippines with me as I needed another doctor. He told me that what he really wanted to do was to go to Africa and do surgery. I asked him to go to Ghana with me to help fill the need there, and he agreed.

Better than that he also decided that he would go to the Philippines with me first, then go to Ghana. He told me that if we were to go, we needed to stay at least a month. I had planned on going for only two weeks, but we compromised on three weeks.

We got in contact with the people in Ghana and they started sending us the required forms for visas and temporary licenses to practice medicine in Ghana. Bud and I found that there were a lot of hoops to jump through, but we proceeded to get all the requirements, like a certified diploma from our medical school, internship, and residency programs, etc.

Dr. Bud Young and I made the Philippines trip. We discussed the trip to Africa and got everything ready that we could. I kept corresponding with Dr. Danny Crawley who was the hospital's only physician and surgeon at the time. I could tell by his emails that he was exhausted and needed help desperately. Danny was instrumental in telling us what we needed as far as supplies, clothes, and what to expect.

The information emailed to us from Danny gave us the history of the Baptist Medical Centre in Nalerigu. The following is from that information:

The first missionary from the Foreign Mission Board (now the IMB) of the SBC arrived in Ghana in 1947. Medical work in northern Ghana was begun using a mobile clinic unit. Years of praying and planning culminated in 1958 when Baptist Medical Centre became fully opened. Dr. George Faile and a few Ghanaian workers began holding daily clinics. Although initially only an outpatient clinic, it was later expanded to include inpatient care, including surgery. The 1960s brought additions to the hospital, including the residential tuberculosis program, which began addressing one of the major health problems in the area.

The 1970s saw further additions for BMC, as well as a serious measles outbreak in the area. In 1978 BMC's medical staff performed an emergency mass immunization of more than 45,000 children. This event opened doors for a strong witness among people otherwise unreached in the area. The hospital's public health program was established the following decade, a work that has allowed a witness to some villages with no evangelical church.

The 1990s brought a crisis that has become a defining event for BMC. In early 1997 an epidemic of cerebrospinal meningitis brought hundreds of extra patients to the hospital. Through the hard work of our staff, government support, Doctors Without Borders, and above all, the provision of our Lord Jesus Christ, BMC emerged from this stressful time stronger than ever. The staff's efforts during the crisis prompted national recognition. Ghanaian President Flt. Lt. Jerry Rawlings honored the hospital with two official visits in 1997 and awarded BMC Ghana's Medal of Honor for its service in the Northern region.

Baptist Medical Centre is located in the village of Nalerigu, in the Northern Region, specifically at 10 degrees 31 N lat. And 0 degrees 22 W long. BMC is a 105-bed hospital (inpatient census often runs 120 or higher) that offers full inpatient services. The clinic is open Mondays, Wednesdays, and Fridays every week except public holidays. In recent years the yearly statistics have been averaging as follows: 60,000 outpatient visits, 10,000 inpatients, 1,000 to 2,000 major operations, and 2,500 to 3,000 minor procedures. Forty churches have been planted as a direct result of the ministries associated with BMC.

Dr. George Faile, Jr.'s wife had breast cancer and had to go home for surgery, radiation, and chemotherapy. The IMB insisted he go with her. Dr. Earl Hewitt had not been on furlough in five years, so he left with his family. This left Danny as the sole surgeon and physician for much of the time. Finally a Ghanaian surgeon was hired for a month to help out.

Bud and I flew from Memphis to Amsterdam to Accra and were met at the airport by Jimmy Huey, Baptist coordinator for Ghana. We spent the night at the Baptist Guest House in Accra and worshiped with a group of Church of Christ folks who were lodging there temporarily. Then it was on to Tamale in the northeast section of Ghana where Danny met us at the airport. It was almost a three-hour drive to Nalerigu from there. Danny was sure happy to see us. He said he had been so busy with little help. For the last couple of weeks he had only a fourth-year medical student, Chuck Barrier from Chapel Hill, North Carolina, to help him. Danny had been forced to essentially stop the clinics during the day and do only emergency surgery. Fortunately, another fourth-year student, Megan Shaw, had arrived to help. They were sharing the general medical call. Except for the recent addition of the Ghanaian surgeon, Danny had all the surgery backup until we arrived.

The drive from Tamale to Nalerigu revealed that the terrain is mostly a wooded savannah with gentle rolling hills. I recognized this as being very similar to other parts of west Africa. Danny said this happened to be the dry season and also some of the hottest weather was approaching. Most of the road was paved all the way to Nalerigu. When we arrived at BMC we went straightway to our guest house which was to be our home for the next three weeks. There we were greeted by Chuck and Megan, who were also happy to see us. They related to us the large amount of work under way and that the clinics would be open the next day since we surgeons had arrived to do elective surgery. Bud had come to repair as many vesico-vaginal fistulas as possible. This type fistula is a connection between the bladder and the vagina caused by prolonged labor with necrosis of the tissues between. This allows a constant drip of urine down the legs—devastating both socially and personally to the person. Dan had found several of these ladies and had them scheduled to come in for elective repair.

The next day, Monday, was extremely busy. According to Chuck, the clinic was packed. Bud scheduled for that week several who had a vesico-vaginal fistula. I scheduled about 8 hernia repairs and general surgery cases. Chuck scheduled a few elective cases as well. By the end of the day we had enough surgery on the elective basis for the entire week. Besides that, the Ghanaian surgeon had scheduled enough cases to occupy one of the operating rooms for the entire week. We had not coordinated our efforts thinking we each would have an operating room.

Danny told us we would be on rotating call, both general medical and backup surgery call. I found out that C-sections were a very common thing there, so I asked Bud to show me how to do C-sections. Where I trained, the ob-gyn docs would not let us do their specialty surgery. So, I watched as I assisted on a C-section on the first day. the next day Bud helped me do an urgent case on a lady with pre-eclampsia and having ineffective labor with her twins. I delivered the first through the incision and Bud rapidly delivered the second.

The next day I was on surgery backup call and was making routine rounds at 8 p.m. when we were called to the delivery suite. The midwives stated that a 21 year-old primi-gravida was not making progress. I suggested an episiotomy and that was done. The baby delivered promptly.

One of the midwives asked me to look at another case that was not progressing. This lady had been in labor all day and had not delivered. On exam she had huge swellings of her vulvae from a very difficult period of labor. The mid-wife told me she probably would not deliver normally. Chuck and Megan said they were going to get Dr. Bud to do a C-section. I reminded them that I was on call and took the initiative to go to the theatre (their word for operating room) as soon as possible. No general anesthesia was available, so we proceeded with Ketamine sedation. A routine operation was started and the baby's head was found to be stuck in the pelvic outlet, but delivered with a little effort. The baby had a low Apgar on delivery, but revived fairly quickly.

When I turned back to the patient, the world had turned red. I soon discovered that she had ruptured her uterus, when we had released the pressure when the baby was delivered through the incision. With a major-emergency prayer and help from Chuck, we sutured the rupture and then the incision site. Chuck said he had never seen that much blood at one time. By that time her blood pressure had dropped to 50/30 and blood was ordered stat. I was told we had no blood bank, but depended on the lab getting blood from relatives or volunteers. We sent three of the immediate family to the lab and within 15 minutes we had two units of typed blood to give. The blood pressure did not respond with fluids until the two units of blood were pumped in. Thank goodness for answered prayers; the mother and baby went home well in five days.

That was a busy day. We as a group did five C-sections in a period of 24 hours. Danny said as far as he knew that tied the record. I was going to help Chuck with one, but he was delayed 20 minutes and I was suturing the skin by the time he could arrive. The theatre was busy all day every day that week as the elective schedule was rolling. We had admitted enough surgery Monday for the entire week.

One of my minor problems was understanding the native Ghanaians with their often broken English. I sure couldn't speak their language.

My first night of primary medical call was greeted about midnight with a very ill 30-year-old lady who had a temperature of 103 degrees. She was delirious, confused, and obviously ill with a stiff neck and severe headache. I did a spinal tap immediately and found she did have meningitis. I used the hospital's protocol and she improved within hours. My word for all this was intense. Bud's term was unrelenting. Bud had been up most of the night he was taking call. He said he could not operate both day and night. After all, Bud is 70-years old. Having found out that Danny had been taking almost all the surgery backup call for nearly three months, I talked with the group and volunteered to take all the surgery backup call if they would cover the medical call. That gave Danny and Bud off every night. Danny said he could get use to that. All this had made me feel inadequate and uncomfortable at all times, so that I trusted in the Lord always, especially with such a large number of ill patients.

The hospital admissions also became very busy; it seems six to eight people were admitted on an urgent basis every night. I made rounds with the primary doc every night to help out and see if any surgery needed to be done. Almost every night I did one or more cases like a ruptured ectopic pregnancy, ruptured appendix, ruptured ileum for typhoid fever, or severe menorrhagia or incomplete abortion (miscarriage) requiring a D&C. The intensity and unrelentingness continued. One night we operated from midnight to 4 a.m. One or two snake bites were being admitted every day or night; but with the hospital protocol not a single one of them died or had serious sequelae.

For anyone who has been to West Africa, they know what I mean: It was warm, as in hot!

We went to prayer meeting on Thursday nights. At one of the missionary's home where the meeting was being held, it was 96 degrees as measured on the wall thermometer. That was at 7 p.m. and by 8:30 p.m. it had cooled all the way down to 95 degrees. Bud took a thermometer one day and placed it over the road surface and it read over 110.

We attended the Second Baptist Church of Nalerigu services on Palm Sunday and Easter Sunday. Those people had a wonderful worship experience each Sunday. We were made to feel very welcome. Another favorable time was using the satellite email to communicate with folks at home; often that was the highlight of my day. I really began to miss my wife and enjoyed getting her emails which arrived almost every day.

Our food was cooked by hired Ghanaians in our guest house and was very tasty. Thank goodness for Crystal Light powder. We had no diet soft drinks. Mary Jane, Dr. Crawley's wife, had us over every Saturday morning for pancakes. I was fortunate enough to have an air conditioner in my room; most of the others did not. Megan said she cooled off at night by placing wet towels on her and letting the fan dry them. Megan and Chuck used my room for a brief nap each day after lunch to rejuvenate after an often all-night call schedule. Chuck and Megan were given and accepted the full responsibilities of a physician and did a great job. What an awesome learning experience for them and whoever would venture to work at BMC!

One Saturday afternoon we got to venture down to the local market where the essentials of living are sold. Food, clothes, and routine things needed in the home abounded in the market place. It was not a souvenir shop, so I did not buy anything.

Before Bud and I left, more recruits were on their way: Dr. Dewey Dunn (gastroenterologist) and Dr. Roy Renfro (general surgeon). Another general surgeon and ob-gyn doctor were to arrive two days after we left.

Dr. Danny Crawley is actively encouraging recruiting help to come to the BMC. If you want a real challenge and rewarding experience, then you need to contact the administration about your wish to serve; they would love to have you come and serve as long as you would like.

I believe Dr. Young (Bud) left happy too. He had done at least a dozen vesico-vaginal fistula repairs. For the first time in years these women were dry—they didn't have a constant stream of urine running down their legs. I felt good about giving Dr. Crawley (Danny) some much needed rest at night for a change. He was so appreciative of our help.

CHAPTER 31

The Conclusion of the Whole Matter

It would only be most appropriate that credit be given where credit is due. Like Solomon in Ecclesiastes 12:13 I have concluded that: "Fear (reverence) God and keep his commandments for this is the entire duty of man." I have found in life that like the song *Trust and Obey*: "trust and obey, for there is no other way to be happy in Jesus."

Jesus paid it all; He died on the cross for my sins. By His blood I am saved. What a Savior!

I want to acknowledge that I serve a great God; that is my comfort. As you have read from the chapters in this book, I have promised Jesus that I would do the Great Commission by doing the Greatest Commandment: "Love the Lord with all your heart, all your soul, and all your mind."

I love Jesus and want to give Him all the honor, praise, and glory in everything that I do. So, this book is written with the attitude of a servant of Jesus. This is the greatest accomplishment in life that I want to obtain now: to be called a friend of Jesus.

CHAPTER 32

Future Missions Planned
Continuing the Call of the Great Commission

As you can see, there has been a metamorphosis of just doing medical mission trips with little or no witnessing to making evangelism the main goal.

At any one given date I usually have plans for a full year or at least three to four trips for future mission trips planned. Frequently I have to turn down good opportunities, but I have to choose which trip fits the need and the group that has the need. It seems that I have specialized in fitting the need of groups that don't have a doctor or one that has had a doctor drop out and needs one to go now. It certainly is more work to coordinate the trip yourself, but doing so is a very rewarding experience when it has concluded.

Throughout the years my favorite trips have been to work with the missionaries in a given country. Opportunities for these seem to arise easily, especially if you are seeking a place to serve. Looking for opportunities on the *IMB.org* (International Mission Board) website and *BMDF.org* (Baptist Medical Dental Fellowship) will have more sites to serve than you can imagine. Missionaries frequently post their need(s) on the website(s). Coordinators such as myself can easily post mission trip(s) there. On my next mission trip I presently have members from five states.

Recruiting for future trips is easiest in your church or with people with whom you have gone on trips before. I have an email list of names on whom I frequently call. Most people I know now are always saying, "Where are you going next?"

I hope this book will give you an incentive to look into going on a mission trip. No greater satisfaction exists than presenting the Gospel to people, especially those that are receptive and hungry for the Word of God, and having them accept Jesus as Savior.

As you have seen, there is also an adventure in every trip. Seeing and blending in with the people of different countries is always an adventure, too. Learning the customs of the people and some of their language is always satisfying.

If you want the blessing of a lifetime or an adventure you will never forget, plan to go on a short-term mission trip. Opportunities abound. You may contact me at *wandvlovejesus@aol.com* and ask, "Where are you going next?"

Photo Album

Above left, William Bailey is pictured during his senior year at LSU medical school in New Orleans 1968. Above right, Bailey is a First Lieutenant in the U.S. Navy. Below, Lt. Bailey flies with his battalion via helicopter to Vietnam,1970.

Dr. William and Vickie Bailey on their wedding day, April 15, 1972.

Lieutenant Bailey as a U.S. Navy physician doing Medical Civilian Action Program (MCAP) work in Vietnam 1970.

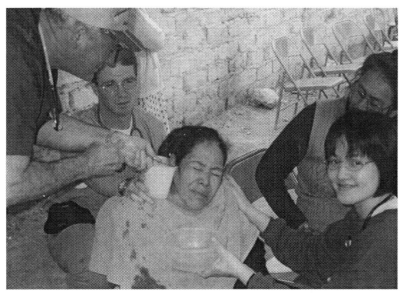

Above Dr. Bailey works with a patient in Mexico alongside LSU medical students (March 1999). Below, Dr. Bailey is pictured with his team in Thailand in November 1999.

Dr. Bailey and his interpreter pictured under mango tree in Burkina Faso 2004.

Dr. Bailey with Rosemary and Buddy Andrews on medical mission August 2000 in Rio de Janeiro, Brazil.

Glen Carter, R.N. and Dr. Bailey after extracting teeth all day in the Philippines.

The medical mission group to Paraguay in 2004 at Iguazu Falls on Brazil side.

At right Dr. Bailey operating at Baptist Medical Centre in Nalerigu, Ghana, April 2006.

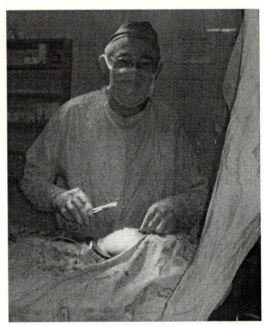

Dr. Bud Young and Dr. Bill Bailey at open market in Nalerigu, Ghana in April 2006.

Phoebe shows her gratitude for the $1,100 gift that our medical team donated to her orphanage for a deep well for safe water. North Benin, January 2005.

Group of 19 pictured in front of Mekong Hotel during medical mission to Kampong Cham, Cambodia. November 2005.

The Plan of Salvation

1. The Bible says that you are accountable for the sin in your life. "For all have sinned and fall short of the glory of God" Romans 3:23.
2. A penalty exists for that sin. "For the wages of sin is death" Romans 6:23.
3. You cannot earn, by good deeds, a way to wipe out that sin from your life. "For it is by grace you have been saved, through faith-and this not from yourselves; it it the gift of God-not by works, so that no one can boast" Ephesians 2:8-9.
4. God provided for your sin by sending His Son to die in your place. Instead of you, Jesus took the wages of sin on Himself by dying on the cross. Then God raised Him on the third day. "But God demonstrates his own love for us in this: While we were still sinners, Christ died for us" Romans 5:8.
5. How do you claim this free gift of Salvation that God has provided? "Everyone who calls on the name of the Lord will be saved" Romans 10:13.

If this makes sense to you then you may pray a prayer similar to this:

"Dear God, Thank You for going to the cross for me. I believe You did it because I am a sinner and You wanted to spend eternity with me.

"Thank You for forgiving me of my sins and giving me a new life. I desire to change my ways and seek a relationship with You. Amen"

Now find a pastor or a Christian friend and tell him or her about your decision.

Order more copies of

You'll Never Run Out of Jesus

Call toll free: **1-877-212-0933**

Visit: www.crosshousepublishing.com

Email: crosshousepublishing@earthlink.net

FAX: 1-888-252-3022

Mail copy of form below to:

CrossHouse Publishing

P.O. Box 461592

Garland, Texas 75046

Number of copies desired _____

Multiply number of copies by $ 15.95

Sub-total _____

Please add $3 for postage and handling for first book and add 50-cents for each additional book in the order.

Shipping and handling $_____

Texas residents add 8.25% sales tax $_____

Total order $_____

Mark method of payment:

check enclosed _____

Credit card# _____

exp. date_____ (Visa, MasterCard, Discover, American Express accepted)

Name _____

Address _____

City State, Zip _____

Phone _____ FAX _____

Email _____

Breinigsville, PA USA
03 December 2010
250602BV00001B/2/A